THE

HOG RANCHES
OF
WYOMING

THE

HOG RANCHES

OF

WYOMING

LIQUOR, LUST, & LIES
UNDER SAGEBRUSH SKIES

LARRY K. BROWN

HIGH PLAINS PRESS

FIRST PRINTING

10 9 8 7 6 5 4 3 2 1

Library of Congress Cataloging-in-Publication Data

Brown, Larry K.
The hog ranches of Wyoming: liquor, lust, & lies under
sagebrush skies / Larry K. Brown
p.   cm.
Includes bibliographical references and index.
1. Bars (Drinking establishments)--Wyoming--History--
19th century.
2. Prostitution--Wyoming--History--19th century.
3. Frontier and pioneer life--Wyoming.
I. Title.
TX950.57.W8B76   1995   95-11823
647.95787'09034--dc20   CIP

ISBN 0-931271-31-2 (cloth : acid-free paper)
ISBN 0-931271-30-4 (soft : acid-free paper)

HIGH PLAINS PRESS
539 CASSA ROAD
GLENDO, WYOMING 82213

DEDICATION

Ruth O. (nee Brown) Dunn...
my mentor and my muse.

CONTENTS

Larry Brown and I first met in 1993 at the Wyoming Department of Commerce where we were both engaged in digging through historic documents. Like explorers in a new land, we were both rediscovering the things that other people knew but which pass out of society's collective memory when individuals die. I guess it was his love of history, and the fact that we had been raised in the same general time period—the 1950s—that made me feel comfortable with Larry, and which led me to ask him if he would like to volunteer his help in producing *Wyoming Annals*. He said he wanted to think it over, but that didn't take long. The next day he said he was amenable to the idea and, in hindsight, I think the suggestion was akin to that of Br'er Bear and Br'er Fox suggesting to Br'er Rabbit that maybe they should throw him into the briarpatch.

An early retiree, Larry has experience in the military, the oil industry and fundraising. Those occupations gave him a general knowledge of a range of subjects and insights into people and social behavior that take a long time to acquire. Combine his experience, his natural curiosity about people and his journalistic background, and you get a storyteller.

It is his inquisitive mind and his interest in the stories of people, particularly those whom others seem to drift past when researching Wyoming and the West, that led me to believe Larry could make a contribution to *Annals*. First, and foremost, he is a capable researcher. "I have my ways," he responds with a mischievous grin when I ask how in the world he digs up the material he finds. His ability to obtain information on any topic is amazing and delightful. A journalistic "nose for news" and an ability to recognize a human interest story and develop its salient points are elements of Larry's current spadework in Wyoming history.

Editor John Charles Thompson, in writing "In Old Wyoming" columns for the *Wyoming State Tribune* from 1937 to 1952, attempted to throw some light on the lives of Wyomingites whose contributions to history he felt deserved to be more widely recognized. Resurrecting Thompson's idea for the *Annals*, Larry Brown also has breathed life in historic personalities which, like old coins, have slipped through cracks in the floorboards of time. Larry's essays are not political or economic histories, nor are they sociological analysis. They are stories. Ultimately, history is story and Larry Brown enjoys the role of storyteller.

The *Hog Ranches of Wyoming* is a collection of stories. When you're done reading this book you may not have learned about the economic importance of the hog ranch in territorial Wyoming society, but you will have tasted a little hog ranch flavor, and partaken of the flesh and blood stories of its denizens. These were people to whom consideration is due, even if formal history passes them by. Avoidance was the rule for most contemporaries of the hog ranch, but sooner or later polite society was affected. An example is Dr. Barber—later a Wyoming governor—who was forced at gunpoint to clean the teeth of a hog ranch proprietor, using the doctor's own toothbrush. When the job was done, the doctor was paid five dollars and both parties were satisfied. You, too, will feel satisfied when you finish Larry Brown's *Hog Ranches of Wyoming* that you learned something about history that doesn't find its way into textbooks.

MARK JUNGE
EDITOR, *Wyoming Annals*

PREFACE

Thanks in great part to the many stories passed down to me about Captain Emmet Crawford, a nineteenth century ancestral hero, I have long been fascinated with the old Indian Wars and tales surrounding them. It wasn't until I seriously began to research the story behind Captain Crawford's capture of "Tousant" Kensler and his subsequent hanging that I learned the most tragic turn in Kensler's sad tale came when he murdered a love rival at a hog ranch. My interest piqued by the incongruous term, I decided to explore its origin and history. In doing so, I quickly learned of the rural hog ranch's inexorable link with the U.S. military and its place in Wyoming's history. Hence, this book.

In writing this story, I am most indebted to Albany County historian and author Elnora L. Frye. Her scholarship and the detail contained in her *Atlas of Wyoming Outlaws at the Territorial Penitentiary* spurred me beyond mere curiosity.

I also wish to express my deep appreciation to the Wyoming Parks and Cultural Resources Division of the Department of Commerce. Most specifically, this book could not have been possible without the help of Jim Donahue's Wyoming State Archives staff. His senior historians Cindy Brown, Curtis Greubel and Carl Hallberg cannot be thanked enough for their invaluable assistance and guidance throughout the project.

Ann Nelson, senior historian with the Wyoming Historical Research Section, too, was a tireless source of suggestions and research support. Paula West Chavoya, supervisor of the Photographic Research Section, and historian LaVonne Bresnahan also were most helpful in producing the necessary photography for this venture.

Others who gave generously of their time, encouragement and expertise in this project are Larry Armstrong, director of the Homesteader's Museum in Torrington, Wyoming; Rick Ewig, Manager/Reference Services at the University of Wyoming's American Heritage Center in Laramie, Wyoming; Mark Junge, editor of the *Annals*, the Wyoming State Historical Society's membership magazine, and Sharon Lass Fields, Wyoming historical researcher and author.

And I especially thank Morris and Sharon Jenkins. Their expert conversion of my computerized copy into a programmed language facilitated its final publication and is deeply appreciated.

Finally, I thank Nancy Curtis and High Plains Press to whom I am most grateful.

LARRY K. BROWN
CHEYENNE, WYOMING

The "Hog Ranch" Defined

"Turn backward. Turn backward,
Oh time in thy Flight.
Make me a cowboy just for tonight
So that I could visit the old
Hog Ranch of Long Long Ago."
ANONYMOUS

 GOOD POETRY, IT IS NOT. This lament, however, does recall a time and place that, like good "likker" or the memory of youth, tends to improve with age.

But what were hog ranches? When did they start? Where are they now?

THE HOG RANCH: ITS ORIGIN & DESCRIPTION

The phenomenon began in the East where our Founding Fathers got stewed on rum and applejack in colonial inns and taverns. Then it crossed the Alleghenies with the settlers and bridged the mighty "Mo" before sailing over the sea of grass into Wyoming and the rest of the West.

The hog ranch was a rural enterprise usually found near military camps and forts where troops were assigned to guard the rail and stage lines from the "hostiles." It was a place where a trooper could while away his off-duty hours with a shot of rye, a game of faro and a roll in the crib with a "soiled angel" made passably attractive by loneliness and miles of sage.

Some saw such a saloon as "a vile robber's roost where the dregs of humanity reveled in swinish drunkeness." It is unlikely, however, that this was why it was called a hog ranch.

A few suggest that because pork was scarce, the government bought it from hog raisers. To put fresh pork on the mess tables in pre-refrigeration times, the critters had to be raised near the army posts, but at an odor-safe distance and, hopefully, downwind from the fort. Writers Willah Weddon and Marion Huseas suggest, "The only women allowed to live on army posts were soldiers' wives and a few laundresses, and then only with special permission of the commandant. So any other women in the vicinity who wanted to be near the troops stayed at hog ranches. The pork raisers faded into obscurity, but the name stuck to centers of ill-repute." A few cynics said that the ranches produced more "'pie-eyed and pickled' pigs than anything else," but it is more likely the only things that were raised in those dens of iniquity were some "hell" and a few bastard babes.

Harry Young, a teamster and frequent visitor of such establishments, speculated: "Why so called, I could not say, as I never saw any hogs around..., but think perhaps it had reference to the girls as they were a very low, tough set." There were even those who said that the people involved in such an unsavory business "moving all the time, created such unsanitary conditions that the name 'Hog Ranch' seemed suitable and fitting."

But perhaps the most credible theory, which has been vouched for by several old timers, is that the term "hog ranch" described the tenderloin girls and their customers: "each of the women had a following of men which resembled an old sow and her numerous little pigs."

SOURCES CITED

Wyoming pioneer Abe Abrahams' correspondence to his Converse County friend Edward F. Rowley provided first-hand memories concerning the hog ranch era and its most colorful characters. Copies of eight letters—written between January 29 and March 21, 1940—on file at the Wyoming Historical Research Section in Cheyenne, WY, offer vivid descriptions of the structures, interior and personalities that came from "having been there." The opening poem was extracted from his February 4 letter to Rowley.

In attempting to determine the origin of the term "hog ranch," the author drew upon a variety of sources: Richard Erdoes' *Saloons of the Old West* (New York: Alfred A. Knopf, 1979); Judy Prosser's "Fort Fetterman Facts: Ranches were Important in Fetterman Days" in the *Douglas* (WY) *Budget* (October 19, 1978); the "Best Little Whorehouse in Wyoming" article by Willah Weddon and Marion M. Huseas that appeared in *True West* magazine (July, 1983); Scott Dial's *A Place to Raise Hell* (Denver: Johnson Publishing, 1977); Harry (Sam) Young's *Hard Knocks: A Life Story of the Vanishing West* (Portland: Wells & Company, 1915); Claude McDermott's "Fort Fetterman & the Old Hog Ranch" in the *Annals of Wyoming* (April, 1964) and J.W. Vaughn's *The*

Fort Laramie Hog Ranches (New York: Westerners N.Y. Posse Brand Books, 1966).

These same sources also were enormously helpful in fleshing out the bleached bones of times and places long gone and nearly forgotten. Dial's book offers a particularly fascinating account about hog ranches in general. It also is an excellent primer on Cheyenne's earliest, steamiest and seamiest history.

Why the Hog Ranch
Grew & Prospered

 FROM 1840 UNTIL NEAR the turn of the century, military posts were built throughout the West to house U.S. Army troops who were brought in to make possible the settlement of the new frontier. Hot on the army's heels came a dedicated group of entrepreneurs who set up hog ranches to provide soldiers, even at the most remote forts, with the "vices of civilization."

Two seemingly unrelated events—the Indian wars and the election of President Rutherford B. Hayes—helped these soldier saloons to grow and prosper.

Until these events, there was no real need for special liquor troughs for soldiers. After all, from the founding of the Continental Army, the American soldier had marched and fought while fortified with liquor that was issued as part of his regular rations. Typical of the times was an order from Fort Sullivan that directed "Nine gills of fatigue rum be delivered to Captain Daniels Company." In addition to those regular liquor rations, special issues often were made in reward for heroic acts. During 1794, Captain Zebulon Pike, who was at that time leading part of General Anthony Wayne's command against the Indians on the Upper Miami River, commended a soldier's bravery and wrote a letter which in part reads, "The bearer of this is entitled to one quart of whiskey having made the best shot on the Left Wing."

The practice of issuing liquor rations continued all through the War of 1812. Old records show that soldiers received regular rations consisting of "meat, bread, salt, vinegar, soap and whiskey."

What was good enough for General Andy Jackson's troops, was intolerable for his soldiers once he had been elected President of the United States. Spirits officially were removed from regular military rations per his directive.

PRESIDENTIAL PROHIBITION

Until the end of President Ulysses S. Grant's administration in March 1877, liquor continued to be available, but only in limited quantities at the forts. Some discretion was expected in the sale of liquor. At most such sites, the sutler, who was authorized by the authorities to sell to or trade with government personnel, had orders to serve drink only every half day to the enlisted men. Violation of that order could result in a sutler losing his license. And so, while the flow of liquor at forts was drastically cut, it was still available for those who could control their thirsts.

After the mid-1860s, military commanders went to considerable effort to curb over-indulgence in alcohol by their men and to control the sources of the supply. They were never completely successful. Liquor could be purchased by soldiers on leave, and it was not unusual for an energetic businessman to pull his whiskey wagon up to the fort boundary, just beyond the reach of the military. Some men stole their alcohol from the hospital and commissary stores.

Soldiers even used blankets and good old fashioned Yankee ingenuity to, what was euphemistically referred to as, "run the mail." Men detailed to work at the washhouse would carry in, amid all the other wet clothes, blankets soaked with whiskey. Once safely past the front gate, they would wring out the potent liquid into pans, then pour the contents into canteens. The punishment for such shenanigans could be severe. One form condemned the guilty, with ten six-pound cannon balls in a knapsack strapped on his back, to march two hours then rest two hours, for fifteen consecutive days and nights.

On February 2, 1881, President Hayes finally signed a bill banning the sale of spirits on all military reservations. The flow may have been cut to a trickle, but the cork still was not in the keg.

It is doubtful that the hog ranches would have become so popular had President Hayes and his administration not been so strict in enforcing its prohibitionist views. In fact, the view that hog ranches were nurtured by the decision not to sell whiskey at the forts is supported by no less than General George Forsyth who said, "the Hog Ranches came about because whiskey could not be sold at the forts." He recalled that as a commanding officer at a post, he ordered the post trader to sell whiskey in violation of regulations. The results: the nearby hog ranches closed within five months and incidents of drunkenness decreased. "The men preferred beer...the attraction of whiskey lay in its unavailability." Wyoming pioneer George Harry Cross agreed. "It [the prohibition] was a terrible mistake," he said, "as drinking had been more or less supervised by the various sutlers. This [abolition of on-post drinking] lead to the creation of tough hog ranches just over the lines of the military installations, that were decidedly demoralizing to many young men."

As the army tried to slake the soldier's thirst with

rules, hard work and heavy-handed discipline, hog ranches sprouted up just beyond the boundaries of military installations to satisfy the troops' desire for booze and other extracurricular activities. Weddon and Huseas wrote, "When a soldier wanted to 'whoop it up' he most often looked for a bottle, a belle and a gaming table." He could always find them at the hog ranch. All the Army commanders could do was try to keep such ranches far enough away to discourage visits by their men, but that distance varied according to the will of the different officers. And the degree of the Army's success was as unpredictable as Wyoming weather.

It is estimated that at the height of the Indian wars more than twenty garrisons were operating in Wyoming, many of which were served by hog ranches. In some cases these establishments were as plentiful as prairie dog towns and were just about as pesky. In fact, a few of the hog ranch proprietors shared a lot in common with such varmints by operating out of holes in the ground. Some ranches, literally, were nothing more than sod huts and cave-like sties carved into hillsides.

OLD MOTHER FEATHERLEGS

One favorite hangout was located between the Running Water and Rawhide Buttes stations (in present-day Goshen County near Lusk, Wyoming) on the Cheyenne-Black Hills Stage Route. It was there in 1876—at the time of General George Crook's Big

Horn and Yellowstone Expedition in pursuit of hostile Indians—that a woman known as "Old Mother Featherlegs" Shephard opened a place of "entertainment" in a dug-out. "A couple of tinhorn gamblers and 'rot gut' whiskey were part of her equipment."

Old Mother Featherlegs, with her great mass of red hair, was so-called because she wore a pair of long red pantalettes that were tied at her ankles. Her dashing about on horseback led one wag to say "them drawers look exactly like a feather-legged chicken in a high wind." As a go-between for the road agents, Featherlegs apparently kept much stolen jewelry and money around her place. About a year after she opened her establishment, Dick Davis (alias "Dangerous Dick the Terrapin," so called "because of a certain hangdog and evil look on his countenance") came to live at her place. He claimed to be a hunter and trapper, but most of his time was spent loafing.

In 1879, Mrs. O. J. Demmon, whose husband owned the Silver Springs road ranch (north of Fort Laramie and between Rawhide Buttes and the present town of Lusk) decided to visit Featherlegs, since she was the only other woman living in the vicinity. Upon arrival, she was horrified to find that Featherlegs had been shot to death while filling a bucket at a spring close to her dug-out. In the nearby soft soil were tracks made by moccasins, the kind of footgear always worn by Dangerous Dick. Neither Dick nor the

$1,500 that Featherlegs was known to have had, was anywhere to be found.

HOG RANCHES COULD BE HAZARDOUS TO YOUR HEALTH

Evidence of the hog ranch's sad impact on the troops is found in a report by the assistant surgeon at Fort Laramie, who wrote in 1869, "The prevailing diseases at the post and vicinity are rheumatic afflictions and venereal diseases, cases of the latter being quite numerous."

In some cases a soldier's visit to a nearby hog ranch resulted in consequences more severe than a case of venereal "drips," a disciplinary dunking in an icy pond or time in the guard house. One trooper fell from his horse in a drunken stupor on his way back to the fort and froze to death. Still another soldier lost his way in bitter weather, gave up in despair and shot himself.

A series of murders was apparently overlooked by the officers at the fort until a soldier was killed at the Six Mile Hog Ranch on July 4, 1867. That incident might have gone unreported, but the hog ranch was pillaged and burned by a company of cavalry sent out to investigate. Concerned that word of that fray might reach the newspapers, Lieutenant Colonel Innis N. Palmer, Fort Laramie's commander, wrote to explain the situation to his superior in Omaha.

Only a month later, Lieutenant Colonel Palmer had to write another letter defending the honor of the fort itself. He had been told the chaplain of Fort Phil Kearny had reported, "The Post at Fort Laramie was a perfect whorehouse." Palmer considered this "a serious reflection upon the officers at this post inasmuch as it represented the moral condition of the post in the most deplorable state," and he said, "there must be some mistake in the matter."

Another post commander came under fire about a month after Fort Fetterman was established. Major William Dye wrote to Lieutenant Colonel Palmer indicating that he, too, was faced with hog ranch problems. "Today, I send a disreputable character en route to Omaha for dealing in whiskey, etc., etc., causing a great deal of trouble amongst the men.

"I have the honor to request that you will furnish her with the necessary transportation and rations to the next post. She is rationed up to the last day of this month." This was the first documented case of illicit female activity at Fort Fetterman, but it would not be the last.

WOMEN WERE SCARCE AS HEN'S TEETH

The importance of women to the hog ranch can be traced as much to their availability as for their "services," because in 1870, the fair sex was as scarce as hen's teeth. There were six men (age twenty-one or more) to every woman of comparable age. George G. McClellan, a pioneer from Big Trails in Washakie

County, recalled that he once went six years without seeing a white woman. "Barbed wire and women," he said, "are the two greatest civilizing agents in the world." In most cases there was little to distinguish the two. While the hog ranch girls could be as sharp and irritating as barbed wire, there were a few men who offered words in their defense. One of the most charitable came from the pen of a frontiersman who wrote: "They [the girls] were a necessary evil. They did little harm—and maybe some good. Many's the man who would never have washed or combed his hair if it was not for thinking of the sporting girls he might meet in the saloon."

Lieutenant John G. Bourke had his own opinion. After visiting the hog ranches in 1877 near Fort Laramie, he wrote: "Three miles [from Fort Laramie] ...there was a nest of ranches, Cuhy [Adolph Cuny] and Scoffey's [Julius "Jules" Ecoffey] and Wright's, tenanted by as hardened and depraved set of witches as could be found on the face of the globe.

"Each of these establishments was equipped with a rum mill of the worst kind and each contained from three to half a dozen Cyprians, virgins whose lamps were always burning brightly in expectancy of the coming of the bridegroom, and who lured to destruction the soldiers of the garrison. In all my experience I have never seen a lower, more beastly set of people of both sexes."

What kind of women lived on the frontier? They were a tough lot. They had to be to survive out there in the late 1800s. But few had a rougher time than the prostitutes. They dealt nightly with drunks, grifters, gamblers and gunfighters and were slapped around with fists and gun butts. And, on the sporting gals' totem pole, the hog ranch hostess was at the bottom. According to one man "A prostitute's standing [so to speak] in her profession depended on her clientele and...when a woman went to the dogs, she went to the soldiers, the lowest level in the customer's scale.... These women were seldom more than vile and diseased whores." And more than a few felt most comfortable when dressed in clothes like the men with whom they slept: boots, canvas pants, military blouses and cast-off uniform hats. They probably took them in trade. Among the more infamous shady ladies, who made her home at the Six Mile and worked the clientele in men's clothes, was Martha "Calamity" Jane Canary. Frills and feathers were few and far between.

There was a poignant side, too, to the lives of the hog ranch women. As historian J. W. Vaughn pointed out, "Lonesome little graves [near the ranch] remain as evidence that some of the women bore children. Despite filth, heat or cold, they must have felt some-thing in these births—if only the pain. Some babies must have lived and...grew up to make their own way in a harsh world" like their mothers.

This tired and trying life did not seem to dampen their feminine instincts. Jealousy, for example, was as easily provoked in them as in any ladies of a church sewing circle. "Al Swearingen rode up to the hog ranch at the head of three wagons loaded with saloon furnishings, including roulette wheels and bonded bourbon, plus a stagecoach full of befrilled and beruffled 'filles de joie.' One of the ranch hostesses, dressed in a drab, faded Cavalry uniform grew so incensed over the advances one of these buxom 'silk sissies' made to a soldier that she pulled a saber and threatened to 'lighten you by your two proudest points if you don't leave 'im alone.'" Old Al decided to protect his assets and quickly hustled his women out of Wyoming and into the Black Hills.

SOME OF THE MORE INFAMOUS HOG RANCHES OF WYOMING

While Old Al skipped to save his skin as well as his "skirts," others sprang like weeds to meet the demands of the soldier, cowpoke, bullwhacker, gambler, road-agent and trail-weary traveler among others left behind. The 1880 Wyoming Territorial census, for example, notes that William (Billie) Brown was the keeper of an inn—the Brown Ranch—in the vicinity of LaPrele Creek, which flowed next to Fort Fetterman. His wife, Ella (Ellie), described herself as the "housekeeper." Their establishment housed at least

Martha "Calamity" Jane Canary, a denizen "dove" of the Six Mile Hog Ranch, often plied her trade in garb discarded by or taken in trade from her military customers. When Calamity was an infant, her father was killed and her mother mortally wounded by the Sioux. Taken to Fort Laramie, she was adopted by a Sergeant Bassett and his wife, and soon became the pet of the garrison. (Wyoming State Museum)

four women whose occupation, according to the census, was prostitution.

George Cross remembers that "We sometimes stopped for a drink at Billie and Ellie Brown's road ranch on Lower LaPrele Creek." Cross recalled, "Ellie was friendly and very nice looking. Cowboys and freighters liked her, and treated her and she apparently drank with everyone." Ellie's good natured advise to customers was "always take your drinks standing up, so you'll know when you've had enough." Sometimes as many as twenty men would treat her within an evening at twenty-five-cents a shot.

It was a mystery to many how Ellie could drink so much and still stay on her feet. One day when Cross and some of his friends were visiting Browns' ranch, he inquired about her secret technique. After some persuading, she confessed:

> When I'm being treated, I always put out two glasses, one for water and one for whiskey. You don't notice it, but the water glass is always empty. When I pour the whiskey into my mouth, instead of swalling [sic] it, I just blow it into the water glass and quickly duck it under the bar.

When Cross joshingly asked her if she sold it to the next customer, she laughed, "Why not!"

A shadow hung over Browns' place that summer as a handsome young newcomer from the East was shot there. He was said to have had considerable money for the purchase of cattle. Some thought he was murdered. Suicide also was mentioned. The Browns claimed he accidentally shot himself while cleaning a gun.

Although the Browns usually managed a relatively "orderly" house, on at least one occasion, they were forced by the local military commandant to mend their ways: "The [Fourth Infantry] Commanding Officer directs that hereafter you close your bar room every evening at 'retreat' the same to remain closed until guard mounting the next morning and that during them hours, you allow no enlisted men in your establishment, or beer to be sold to them."

A "Madame" W. Selig operated the Nine Mile Ranch, the first road ranch and stage stop north of Cheyenne, where she built a large dance hall with sleeping quarters upstairs, thereby offering her patrons a wider variety of entertainment and hospitality.

There were other popular, but less publicized, hog ranches such as an unidentified haunt in the vicinity of Fort McKinney. The Cantonment McKinney on Powder River also had its house of entertainment. Although fairly inaccessible now, it was only a short way from the main trail down the Dry Fork of Powder River. The story handed down is that the post traders in the area backed the hog ranch, but concealed their ownership.

And then there was Sarah Petite, who had a small rural "pay and play" operation outside Chugwater as well as John Curtis and J.A. Gordon, who managed a string of eight girls at their hog ranch near Rawlins in June 1880. Another "ranch" was established in that vicinity in early 1877 a few hundred yards off the Fort Fred Steele reserve. It was situated on the left bank of the Platte River a few miles below the fort, according to correspondence from the commanding officer, Captain Henry E. Noyes.

Just north of Laramie, along the rail line of the Union Pacific, Mary and Ed Brady operated a ranch/brothel business in the 1870s to entertain the Fort Sanders enlisted men as well as other in the area. Although no names of resident prostitutes were linked to Mary Brady, as early as 1872 she was charged with "keeping a common, ill-governed and disorderly house to the encouragement of idleness, drinking and fornication." Between 1872 and 1875, Mary ran afoul of the local authorities on various occasions until she faced the district court on the charge of threatening the life of one Thomas Dillon.

One of the lesser known establishments of this type was the one that was operated on the "Flats" near Wheatland where the Wyoming Development Company was constructing an irrigation ditch in 1894. The business was managed by a "madam" from Denver who had four girls working for her until one bleak and blustery March day in 1894. Babe, one of the "ranchhands," ended it all by drinking carbolic acid. There was no undertaker in the area, but a "Mr. McCallum," who ran a local lumberyard, supplied a pauper's casket. He and his wife loaded the "flimsy, cheaply-constructed burial box, shaped like a violin case and covered with sleazy black outing flannel" into the back of their horse-drawn wagon.

Given the time of the year, lack of greenery and Mrs. McCallum's sympathy for the girl, she cut the one tall stalk with three flame-colored bells from her prized amaryllis plant and gathered a half-dozen leaves from her Boston fern for the ceremony. Then, together, the McCallums set off to deliver the deceased to the ditch camp saloon where the bartender agreed to host the funeral.

Arriving at the pub, Mr. McCallum wrapped Babe's body in a discarded tarp before placing it in the coffin which he had perched atop three empty beer kegs at the far end of the saloon. Mrs. McCallum, in the meantime, spotted a guitar hanging back of the bar. The saloon handyman could have played it, but he had been sent to dig Babe's grave. A patron there volunteered to sing "Jesus Loves Me, This I Know"—the only song in his repertoire—while Mrs. McCallum delivered the eulogy. It didn't take long, because Babe was the only name the girl used and no one knew from whence she came. In closing, the well-intentioned Mrs.

McCallum struggled to recall the Bible story of the woman taken in sin. Finally, she reminded those assembled, "He that is without sin among you, let him first cast a stone at her." The service was ended. The coffin was returned to their wagon and within minutes was lowered into the cold grave in a lonely spot back of the camp. The only marker on the fresh-turned earth was a bright red amaryllis spray embraced by dark green fern fronds and tied together with a ribbon from a box of candy.

Sources Cited

To explain why the hog ranches grew and prospered, the author again relied extensively on Prosser's account of Fort Fetterman as well as Dial's history of saloons in Wyoming. Also quite helpful were Eugene K. Galloway's "Hog Ranches were Soldiers' Source for Brew and Witches" in the *Torrington* (WY) *Telegram*, (June 23, 1966), and Weddon and Huseas's previously mentioned well researched and written story in *True West*. Anecdotes from Francis Paul Prucha's book *Broadax & Bayonet* (Lincoln: University of Nebraska Press, 1953) were helpful, too, in illustrating the typical soldier's "Yankee ingenuity" when it came to satisfying his baser needs. Unexpected insight regarding the relationship between hog ranches and military installations came from Herbert Hart's *Old Forts of the Northwest* (Superior Publishing, 1963).

Still other vignettes concerning some of the most infamous pay and play establishments were taken from Maurine Carley's fascinating compilations of "Trek" tales as told in the Wyoming Historical Society's *Annals*. For example, Bob Darrow tells the memorable story of Old Mother Featherlegs Shephard in "Cheyenne-Deadwood Trail Trek" (April, 1965). Carley's "Oregon Trail Trek No. One" (October, 1955) also was very helpful.

Additional details concerning Mother Featherlegs came from Bill Barnhart's nomination of the Cheyenne-Black Hills Stage Route Historic Area submitted by the Wyoming Recreation Committee to the National Register of Historic Places, U.S. Department of the Interior, National Park Service (Entry #69-04-49-0001, April 16, 1969).

The author is indebted, too, to Anne M. Butler for her wonderful stories about the poor "Cyprians" and much maligned *Daughters of Joy, Sisters of Misery* (Chicago: University of Chicago Press, 1984). Lieutenant John Bourke's description of those denizens came from that source.

And there is probably no one more expert in or more understanding of Wyoming territorial history than Agnes Wright Spring. She describes with conviction and authority *The Cheyenne & Black Hills Stage & Express Route* (Glendale, CA: Arthur H. Clark, 1949).

A frequently overlooked, but enormously valuable research source is the early Wyoming Census records that are available for study at the Wyoming Historical Research and Publications Section at the Barrett Building in Cheyenne, WY. The 1870 and 1880 records provided names, dates, addresses, occupations and nativities that are not available through any other sources.

Military Post Returns, Medical Histories, Letter-books, Letters Received, which also are too frequently overlooked, added flavor to this book. The military records referred to in this book are archived at the Wyoming State Museum. An obscure January 18, 1887, letter from an unknown Fourth Infantry Second Lieutenant, who served as the Post Adjutant at Fort Fetterman to hog ranch proprietor William H. Brown, explains, for example, how the military maintained order when its rules were violated.

And, of course, *John Hunton's Diaries, 1873-1884* as edited by L.G. Flannery (5 vols.; Lingle, WY: *Lingle Guide-Review*, 1956-64) are "must reads" by any student of Wyoming history. Details regarding the Brady's ranch/brothel business near Fort Sanders came from a segment reprinted in the *Lingle* (WY) *Guide-Review* (July 14, 1955).

The Wild Bunch Visits
Anderson's Hog Ranch

BEFORE RELATING A FEW anecdotes about the most notorious hog ranches in the state, I would be remiss if I didn't share a pioneer's recollections about the liquor, lust and lies he witnessed at "Bad Land Charlie" Anderson's hog ranch. Charlie and his brother Lyman came west from Illinois in the late 1880s and homesteaded about a half a mile east of Thermopolis. It was on the east bank of the Big Horn River near the mouth of Owl Creek in the green crescent valley that they built their homes of cottonwood logs some two feet thick.

The Anderson brothers were considered a little on the shady side and played host periodically to outlaws and rustlers who, if they got into trouble in Fremont County on the west side of the river, could splash east across the stream into what was then Johnson County and out of reach of the law. Although Charlie's place was one of the least known establishments of its kind, its very anonymity seems responsible, at least in part, for attracting its most infamous clientele: the Wild Bunch.

After that gang placed a red lantern on the tracks to flag down the Overland Flyer on June 2, 1899, near Wilcox, Wyoming, they cracked its safe with dynamite. Then dragging sacks of twenty dollar notes, they escaped to Anderson's Hog Ranch. It was there that Harry "The Sundance Kid" Longabaugh; Harvey "Kid Curry" Logan; the Perry boys; "Jumbo" McKenzie, "big, blundering" Tom O'Day, and others of the gang split their swag.

It was while they were holed up at the ranch that they sent word via Pete Mickelson, a stage driver and mail carrier, to the "Sagebrush Dentist" Dr. Will Frackelton in Sheridan to come "and look their teeth over." It is from the doctor's first-hand account of his visit there with his partner, "a bespectacled Quakerish" optician, that we have one of the most colorful accounts of life at a hog ranch.

Frackelton recalled that on his stage ride there with Pete, he asked about their destination, Anderson's Hog

Ranch. "I didn't know they raised hogs in this country," Frackelton commented. Pete gave him a long, sidewise glance before answering. "Doc, there's a lot o'things hain't in the books yet."

That afternoon they passed through desolate country filled with alkali dust and sage that in some places grew as high as a man's head. Unexpectedly, the stage rounded a big red butte near the bluffs of the Big Horn River and nearly bumped into a log store that served as a post office and trading place. Frackelton's partner, the optician, who was following in their buckboard, pulled to a stop in the dusty shadow of the stage.

Across the river was a long, low building roofed with red shale in which a few weeds had sprouted. Each window held four stained panes of glass that looked like they had never been opened or washed. Jokingly, Doc Frackelton swung his thumb towards the building as Pete climbed down from his wagon. "That the hog ranch?"

"Maybe so," said Pete before entering the store with his mail sack. While they waited, strains of music drifted across the river.

"Sounds like a piano," Frackelton suggested as Pete returned to get some goods from the stage.

"Just what it is," he answered. "First one ever freighted into the Big Horn Basin. Hain't you goin' over? You'll find some of the boys (the Wild Bunch) there."

Rejoining his partner in their buckboard, Frackelton and the optician forded the river and rode up to the front door of the rambling five-room building. At one end of the long, dimly lit room was a bar of rough pine. Along the wall behind it were a few dusty glasses and a mirror decorated with soap frost by some wandering amateur artist. At each end of the bar was a box filled with sawdust although the floor was proof the customers had been none too expert in hitting the makeshift cuspidors. The bartender, in his shirt sleeves, sported a big moustache and a cowlick of hair, brushed carefully down over his low forehead. The piano was in the corner, its case well scarred by cigarette burns and rings left by liquor glasses. Over its battered keys drooped "Professor" George Carwile, who was playing for his own amusement. The once promising university graduate and talented musician had fallen to the lowly level of a barroom thumper.

The barkeeper, looking up, greeted the men with "How," and pushed a bottle of whiskey towards Frackelton and his friend before returning his attention to the glass he had been polishing. Now and then he looked over the end of a big, black cigar that hung from a corner of his mouth as Frackelton moved towards a table where a Mexican monte game was in progress. A one-armed card sharp dealt while several cowboys eyed their hands. As was the style, some stood while others hung their hips on the edge of the table. Their bets were mostly in new, crisp twenty dollar bills not usually found in the possession of forty-dollar-a-month cowpokes.

"Bad Land Charlie" Anderson's Hog Ranch Saloon was a favored spa for the "Wild Bunch" members who, if they got into trouble with the law on one side of the Big Horn River, splashed across to the other side and into the adjoining county. (Hot Springs County [Wyoming] Museum)

As the dentist returned to the bar, the bartender grew confidential. "Doc," he said, "the boys are gettin' a little careless about them twenties. Took 'em in the last Union Pacific deal and some ain't signed up. If you get aholt of any like that, bring them to me and I'll give you signed ones."

Suddenly guns began to crack outside. "Shootin' for the drinks," the bartender explained.

"Private affair?" asked Frackelton.

"Guess they'll let you in, kid," the barkeeper replied with a wry smile.

Exiting the shack, Frackelton could hear the shots coming from up river, so before joining in, he went back to the buckboard where he donned a garish, old derby hat that he had tucked away in his bedroll. He moved toward the noise with a .45 in his belt. No sooner had he been greeted by the rowdy outlaws than Harry Longabaugh, best known as the "Sundance Kid," snatched the dentist's derby and threw it high in the air while the Wild Bunch blazed away without success. Grabbing the Sundance Kid's Stetson, Frackelton asked, "Will you give me a chance in return?" Apparently amused by the visitor's nerve, the Sundance Kid nodded his approval. "Old Man Colt was working for me," the dentist recalled later, "and I drilled the hat." "It's better ventilated now," he kidded the Kid; "you shouldn't get hot-headed."

Returning their attention to the earlier shooting contest, the participants tossed their ante of silver dollars on a blanket that had been stretched on the turf. Then with a shrill, nasal "High-Yah," a gang member threw a chunk of wood into the fast moving Big Horn. As the swift current caught the wood and spun it about, it required a sure eye and calm hand to score a hit. Each man in turn drew a bead and fired. The first to make the chips fly was the winner, who plucked the money from the blanket to pay for the drinks that followed each round. "I'm afraid I wasn't thinking much about dentistry by the time the cook sounded the triangle and yelled 'Come an' get it or I'll throw it out,'" Doc Frackelton remembered.

As they staggered down to supper while singing snatches of a ribald cowboy song, big Tom O'Day remarked that they were in for some fine eating. "Wan av th' byes brought in a slow elk," he explained. [A "slow elk" was a branded yearling steer or heifer from which all evidence of ownership had been removed.]

"Well," Frackelton observed, "I suppose you hung the hide on the fence properly so the brand inspector could tally it."

Shaking his head, O'Day bemoaned, "One Gut's been gettin' danged fergetful here o' late. Sure must remind him to do that."

One of the Perry boys joined into the conversation. "Hell, Doc," he protested, "that critter was way off'n Otto Frank's range anyhow. Otto won't miss him and we gotta have our meat. Them Pitchfork [ranch] cowpokes had no business lettin' him stray."

"Just the same," interjected McKenzie, "he should-n't 'a done it. Not with the biggest outfits in the country payin' their top ropers five dollars per head to lay a runnin' iron on any maverick or stray critter they find. Only trouble is, some o' the boys are a little too independent. They're buildin' up nice little herds for themselves and that don't set so good with the range bosses."

"You don't say!" Perry retorted.

"Hell, yes," McKenzie rumbled on. "Look at old McNaffy in Gillette. He got way out ahead and had the goods on the range boys, so what did they do but give him two years' wages to stay in town and keep his trap shut. Sure, One Gut is gettin' careless."

Entering the messhouse, the tipsy gunsels and their guests found a surprise. Mag Jess, who ran one of the most notorious brothels in Buffalo had come visiting with some of her girls. Although the doves were a bit over the hill and more than a little soiled, their cracked smiles and loose-fitting Mother Hubbards attracted plenty of attention. "You see, Doc," said O'Day a bit thickly, "it ain't style they're after wit' them things. It's th' fresh air they like. Just wait till you see 'em tonight. They sure put on th' scenery."

Although Frackelton by that point was well into the party, his sober partner kept giving him dour looks. As soon as they had finished the meal, the optician insist-ed they leave the bar for a private talk. Once out of earshot the optician warned the well-juiced dentist he feared they had been lured to the ranch so that the gang could roll them for their poke. "Listen, Frackelton," he said earnestly, "hasn't Tom (O'Day) the reputation of being the tipoff man for the gang around Sheridan?"

"Yes."

"Don't you suppose he heard about your plans to return home this winter?"

"Well...maybe."

"How many times did Big Tom bump up against you in the messhouse?"

"He'd just had a drop too much."

"Or was he trying to learn where you carried your money," persisted Frackelton's friend. "Oh, you needn't start laughing again. It won't be such a joke after they've taken our summer's earnings.... Didn't they send for you through Pete Mickelson?"

"Yes."

"Wanted you to look over their teeth, didn't they...? Well, has even one of them so much as mentioned a toothache...? I tell you, we're in a trap and we've got to get out of it."

As his head began to clear, Frackelton finally acknowledged his partner's suspicions made sense. "What'll we do?"

"Pull out of here right now."

But a sudden departure, they feared, would never do. It would attract attention. They would be followed and overtaken. A plan of escape evolved. Frackelton would wear his derby hat and act the life of the party by trying to drink the bunch down. The optician would play sick, stay in their camp and when the time was right, harness the team for a fast getaway at dawn. The horses were to be watered and given a good feed of hay and oats. Just before starting, they were to be given an extra measure of oats but no hay. The optician would pick up Frackelton at dawn, and they'd take to the road. In case Frackelton was incapacitated, his partner was to drive slowly for the first five miles and then to go as fast as possible until they reached Lost Cabin on the stage route to Casper. If they reached there safely, the more able-bodied of the two was to board the stage to Casper where he was to put their earnings in a bank for safe-keeping.

To aid the illusion, the two men returned to the bar where the optician asked for a drink of Jamaica ginger, the panacea for most ills in those days. After taking the drink, the "ailing one" was escorted by Frackelton back to their camp. There the dentist started a small fire and fried some bacon as he shifted the skillet from side to side to let the grease cool.

"What's the idea?" asked his partner.

"The fire's to keep you warm," Frackelton grinned. "What could be more natural? As for the grease, Sam Stringer, the mule skinner, once said that if you greased your in'ards, you could drink any son of a bachelor down.... Brother, I have work to do tonight and not only sons but daughters of bachelors to outdrink," he added. Handing his .45 to the optician, Frackelton told him to "Hang onto this unless it's needed. I'm going to outsmart them empty-handed."

By the time Frackelton had returned that night to the hog ranch dance hall, the girls had gone to great lengths per O'Day's prophesy to put the "scenery" on. The skimpy clothes they wore offered a generous peek at feminine charms, and the more coquettish of the girls affected baby talk to woo their "sugar daddies."

In the meantime, Carwile took his place at the piano while One Gut, the lean Texan and donor of the slow elk, prepared to call the dance that was about to start. Shortly before the show, two Hungarian troubadours, attracted by the noise, drove up with a rickety old wagon pulled by a team of cayuses. One musician carried a bass drum and cymbals while the other sported a cymbalon that was shaped like a zither, but about three times as long. After arguing briefly with Carwile over remuneration, they finally reached an agreement. Down went the instruments beside the piano and into a wild Czardas went Carwile and his new-found band. The Hungarian with the cymbalon hammered away with two knobbed sticks while the drummer imitated the roll of thunder. Carwile, the versatile, followed on the piano.

In the midst of the tune, One Gut yelled, "This hain't no concert; hit's a dance. Grab a dressmaker an' let's get goin'."

"Oy, yoi, Doc, come on an' get in the first set," screamed a girl called Goldie as she grabbed the dentist's derby. "Let's start things."

It was a square dance and within a few minutes all the available women were taken. Since the men were in the majority, two of them tied their handkerchiefs around their arms and played the woman's part. One Gut bawled, "Gent's salute your ladies" as Carwile beat out "The Arkansas Traveler." Stepping smartly in time to the tune, each dancer offered his own interpretation of the dance as One Gut sang out:

> All join hands and balance and swing,
> The crow flies out and the bird flies in.
> All join hands and dance and swing,
> Chase the duck with the golden wing.

Another call was:

> Captain Jinks of the horse marines,
> Then to the boy that carries the beans.

At the end of the dance, the Texan prodded the men to "Take your ladies to the bar and don't ferget the professor." Accordingly, as each man passed Carwile he threw two-bits into an old phonograph horn put there for that purpose. At the bar whiskey went for fifty cents a pop while each woman received a short beer plus a check for her time which went promptly into her cloth purse.

In addition to the square dances, they waltzed to such favorite melodies as "After the Ball" and "Over the Waves." The surprise hit of the evening turned out to be Frackelton's derby which the bartender insisted on wearing each time he served the dentist and his partner, Goldie. The musicians and girls, too, took turns under its battered brim. The last anyone recalled, however, was that the hat was atop One Gut's head while he yelled lustily, "Oy, yoi, yoi."

As the hour grew late, couple after couple passed out of the small hall, but it was a personal matter and no questions were asked. All except Frackelton who declined the boudoir invitations, explaining he was "full of bad whiskey and good resolutions, and preferred the dance, the music and more whiskey to the pleasures of seclusion."

As the first gray streaks of dawn blushed in the east, Frackelton could only recall sharing one last drink with Mag Jess, the caller, and the musicians. "I remember," he said, "that Mag Jess swayed slightly and grew more openly amorous in her invitations." It was then, fortunately, that his partner, according to their prearranged plans, appeared in the doorway of the dance hall. But after that, everything went blank.

When he came to, he felt and heard their little team of Morgans pounding smoothly along the road as if they knew how much depended upon them. "Oh, what a head! And the sun beating down on it! My arms," he claimed, "were hanging between my knees and I felt a constriction about my waist. It was the halter rope holding my swaying body to the buckboard seat." As his partner's laugh broke through the aching mist, Frackelton asked, "Did you give the team the light feed of oats?"

"Yes."

"How long have we been on the road?"

"Couple of hours," he laughed again.

"Go ahead," Frackelton said. "Have your little joke. You've earned it. They can never catch us with this start."

Scenery, heat, dust, thirst, and hunger were forgotten as they raced along, stopping only once to let their team drink sparingly. As luck had it, they reached Lost Cabin just as the Casper stage pulled in. There was no argument as to who was in better condition for the journey, so the optician climbed aboard with their savings and left in a cloud of dust.

After taking care of the team of Morgans and eating a little, Frackelton took a much needed siesta. Waking, he saw, far off on the Hog Ranch Road, an eddy of dust that drew nearer. A short time later, Tom O'Day flung himself off his horse before the door of the Lost Cabin Saloon and approached the dentist. "Howdy, Doc," he said cheerily, but with a businesslike look in his eye. "What, only wan av yez?"

"You're a little too late, Tom. He left on the stage for Casper some time ago. And if it's our poke you're after, my partner took it along with him."

Tom blinked, then threw back his head and laughed. "Shure, Doc, I told th' byes you were too fast for us. Th' drinks are on me." Then, winking slyly and lowering his voice confidentially, he asked, "We're needin' th' likes av yez wid us. Howja like to join up?"

History failed to record his reply.

Sources Cited

The wonderful first-hand account regarding the Anderson Hog Ranch by Dr. Will Frackelton would not have been possible without the trusting relationship between the doctor and author Herman Gastrell Seely. Please note that the quotations and dialogue of the characters, like those throughout this book, are verbatim from the original source text.

For additional details regarding Dr. Frackelton and his misadventures in the Old West, the reader is encouraged to read Seely's book entitled, *Sagebrush Dentist* (Pasadena, CA: Trails's End Publishing, 1947). Also, for an interesting but somewhat flawed account of the Wilcox train robbery, James D. Horan's book *Desperate Men* (New York: G.P. Putnam's Sons, 1949) will help put in perspective the Wild Bunch's visit at Anderson's. Supplemental information was obtained from a variety of news clippings and memoirs provided by the Hot Springs County Museum and Cultural Center in Thermopolis, Wyoming.

The Six Mile Hog Ranch

 PROPRIETORS AND CUSTOMERS of hog ranches usually were more pragmatic than imaginative about naming those dens of iniquity. The haunts of Brown, Brady, and Anderson, for example, bore the names of their owners or operators. Most such labels, however, were determined by the establishment's distance from the nearest military post. And, of the many "resorts" found in those days across wide, wild Wyoming, few historians dispute that the Six Mile, Three Mile and One Mile hog ranches were by far the most notorious. The Six Mile, for example, that served Fort

Laramie, from its inception in 1849 until its abandonment forty years later, was "six miles southwest of Fort Laramie, on Baptiste Fork."

It is not known exactly when the Six Mile was built, but a soldier could get all the action he wanted there. The owners served meals, stocked a good selection of liquor and cigars and usually had in residence a half-dozen of the vilest sort of prostitutes. The only hitch was that a written pass was required for a soldier to be more than a mile from the flagstaff. Many men took their chances as evidenced by trials recorded in the garrison's Post Returns.

The first reference to the Six Mile in the Fort Laramie post records appears in February 1867. An army messenger found a mail escort party at the ranch supposedly headed for Fort Phil Kearny, imbibing freely of the proprietor's liquid wares. Two soldiers lay drunk by the door, and the messenger reported the rest of the party huddled inside in a similar condition. A short time later, April 21, 1867, Sergeant Kesner of Company A, Second Cavalry, decided to take on the Six Mile in style. The officers who later sat in judgment decided that his "borrowing" an ambulance with a team and then returning roaring drunk was simply going too far. Kesner forfeited his stripes and ten dollars of his pay.

Later there was Private William McCormick, Company E, Ninth Infantry, who left the post without permission one evening in April 1876, to go on a spree. When he returned the next afternoon about one, still inebriated, he may have had some regrets. The night out cost him twelve dollars and twenty days of hard labor.

In many instances, the effects of over-indulgence were much more serious. In 1877, two Third Cavalry soldiers, Privates McGuire and Browne, tangled in one of the resorts near the fort. During the fight, McGuire shattered a bottle over Browne's head. Then, seizing a second one, continued to beat Browne until he was severely injured. On another occasion, a Fifth Cavalry trooper, John Robinson, fell drunk from his horse, caught his foot in the stirrup and was dragged. Before the horse could be stopped, Robinson's skull was crushed.

The fact that some soldiers would drink almost anything that unscrupulous ranch owners would sell sometimes proved tragic. A Seventh Infantry private, James Collins, serving at Fort Laramie in 1887 was found dead off post. An autopsy determined the cause of his death was alcoholic poisoning.

Similar actions by Fort Laramie soldiers brought a ruling from their Commanding Officer that same November that John Hunter, the owner of the Six Mile, discontinue the sale of liquor to soldiers or lose his trader's license. In December, he was told to destroy all alcoholic beverages in his possession. Hunter ceased to be a problem in October 1868, when Bud Thompson removed him permanently from

The Fort D.A. Russell guardhouse, shown here at the right tip of the "diamond in the dust," housed John Boyer and Tousant Kensler before they became the first two men legally hanged in Wyoming. Their crimes? Boyer bid two fellow Six Mile Hog Ranch customers farewell with a seven-dollar revolver while Kensler killed a rival for the favors of a Six Mile whore. (Courtesy Wyoming State Museum)

the scene with the aid of a revolver—the first man to be murdered at the Six Mile.

Hunter's death, unfortunately, would not be the last. George Blake was arrested by Sheriff T. Jeff Carr for an assassination at Six Mile Ranch in 1872. At least seven more men died in gun fights there during the next nine years.

JOHN BOYER: WYOMING'S FIRST LEGAL VICTIM OF THE NOOSE

Two years later—on October 27, 1870—John Boyer bid two local Six Mile customers farewell with a seven-dollar revolver. He fired one lead slug into William H. Lowry's left breast and put a second round into the gut of James McClusky.

The trouble started when young John Boyer came home and found his widowed Sioux mother and sister tied and gagged. They had been raped by the two men, who were known to hang around Fort Fetterman. The next night, October 30, Boyer encountered the rapists at a dance that was held at the Six Mile ranch. He was unarmed, however, because the bartender had taken each patron's weapons for safekeeping as he entered the hall.

Waiting until about 2 A.M., Boyer retrieved his pistols from the barkeep and left the building. Soon after, he mounted his horse and rode back to the entry where he called for McClusky and Lowry. He called them out saying "he could whip them." As they appeared at the door, the twenty-six-year-old pulled his revolver and "deliberately, and without a moment's warning, shot and killed them both." Boyer immediately fled—undeterred—and hid with a band of local Sioux. However, the Indians, fearing reprisals, turned him over to the authorities when they demanded his return.

While waiting for the First District Court, which had convened to decide his fate, Boyer threatened to foil the noose when he escaped on or about March 30, 1871, from the Fort D.A. Russell guard house where he was kept pending his execution. The three-hundred-dollar reward that was offered for his capture was claimed several days later as he was arrested enroute back to Fort Laramie.

"He was met on the road walking alone with his handcuffs off and fastened to his belt," witnesses reported. "Seeing the coach coming, he left the road, and while the stage was passing a curve in the road, hiding him from view, he secreted himself under the bank of a ravine, and was only discovered and recognized as the stage had passed his place of concealment." Fort Laramie officials quickly sent a "Captain Wilson" and a detachment of Fifth Cavalry soldiers, who raced to the spot armed and ready. Boyer would not refuse the captain's "invitation" to join them for a trip back to Cheyenne. Authorities put him on the

"Tousant" Kensler was imprisoned for a short time in the guard house at Fort Laramie before he was transferred to Cheyenne where he was tried. The structure held about two dozen prisoners in an unheated and unlighted substory room. There was no furniture. Bedding consisted only of the blankets which prisoners brought with them. Kensler was accused of murdering a rival for the affection of one of the "girls" at the Six Mile Hog Ranch. He was subsequently found guilty and became the second man legally hanged in the Wyoming Territory. (Wyoming State Museum)

next stage to Cheyenne where he arrived Sunday evening, April 2.

The young felon, having had no food for four days for fear of being recognized by ranchers in the area, was "half famished...and partook with eagerness of the lunch which was offered" by the soldiers. His feet also were badly frozen and very painful.

Back in jail and "heavily ironed," Boyer amused himself during the long, lonely hours by sketching. A reporter for the *Cheyenne Daily Evening Leader*, who saw the drawings, was impressed with his artistic skill. He said Boyer "made a very creditable portrait of himself suspended from the gallows, the court room, the judge who pronounced the sentence, and the jury which found him guilty of murder. In his picture of the jury, he gives the lady members...a horrid appearance. Boyer either has no eye for womanly beauty, or else he is opposed to women's rights."

As evidenced during his final moments, Boyer did not hold women in high esteem. The *Evening Leader* reported he went to meet his Maker on April 21, 1871, in an "old grout building, nearly in front of the jail" in Cheyenne with these words on his lips: "Look at me! I no cry, I no woman; I man. I die brave!"

Boyer had the "distinction" of being the first of only seven persons to be legally hanged in the Wyoming Territory.

Captain Emmet Crawford, Third Calvary, and Lieutenant P.H. Ray, Eighth Infantry, captured the murderous "Tousant" Kensler at the Red Cloud Agency in Nebraska Territory after he had escaped from Fort D.A. Russell's guard house near Cheyenne. Crawford had his brains blown out—literally—in 1886 by bandits while leading a military expedition into Mexico in pursuit of Geronimo. (Courtesy Captain Crawford's niece, Mrs. Ruth O. (nee Brown) Dunn; Fort Collins, CO)

"Tousant" Kensler Shoots
a Sheep Herder

A second murder took place at the Six Mile on April 9, 1872, when Adolph Pena, a Mexican sheepherder took a Winchester carbine slug through the entire width of his body. A love rival, William "Tousant" Kensler fired the shot at the height of a jealous fit over one of the "fallen angels" who worked there at the bar.

Kensler, a hunter of German and Indian heritage from Iowa, and his seventeen-year-old wife, Mary, had two children at their home near Fort Laramie, but the twenty-three-year-old Romeo had a yen for Jennie Hogan, who worked at the hog ranch.

The evening probably started quietly enough as customers drifted off the trail and into and out of the bar. Suddenly Kensler and Pena found themselves in the same room—at the same time—with their lover. As words grew more personal and heated with each drink, Pena "sneeringly taunted" Kensler about his relationship with the bar girl they shared. Kensler's rage and retorts were equally provocative.

Suddenly, Pena broke from the room and headed upstairs where he donned his revolver. Through the dim, flickering light cast by the oil lamps that hung from the rough hewn beams, Kensler could see Pena returning with iron on his hip. Sensing the danger, the young Kensler quickly left the bar. Angry and embarrassed at being "skedaddled," he pulled a twenty-dollar

Winchester carbine from the scabbard on his horse's saddle and returned to the side of the building. Standing at a window, Kensler fired a slug that ripped a one-inch wound in Pena's left side, burying itself some twelve inches deep, coming to rest under the skin on the far side of his lean body. Pena died the next day. That act, Kensler later claimed, was as spontaneous as it was fatal.

Kensler was captured the next day at the Three Mile Hog Ranch by a military pursuit detachment headed by Captain E.R. Wells, Company E, Second Cavalry, out of Fort Laramie.

He subsequently was tried and sentenced to hang, but escaped the Laramie County jail and fled to "Indian Country" near the Red Cloud Agency in Nebraska. There he painted his face and disguised himself in Indian garb to avoid detection. However Lieutenants Emmet Crawford, Company G, Third Cavalry, and Patrick Henry Ray, Eighth Infantry, found and captured him after shooting him through both legs near Little Wound's Oglala Sioux encampment.

The military returned Kensler to Cheyenne where on November 19, 1874, he became the second person legally hanged in the Wyoming Territory.

BEWARE AN UNSAFE HARBOUR

Still another man, Perry Harbour, a wood-cutter, took a lead ball in the gut at the Six Mile on August 13,

1871, after getting drunk and intimidating some of the customers there in the bar. He died the following day.

His trouble had started three or four days earlier near the sutler's store at Fort Laramie when he pulled his revolver on a twenty-year-old blacksmith named George W. Blake. Although Harbour holstered the weapon without hurting anyone, he warned Blake he would put a slug through him "before a week went over his head." However, few seemed to believe that his abuse was anything more than "Dutch courage" at work.

Nonetheless, they met again unexpectedly the following Sunday outside the Six Mile saloon where Harbour was threatening the life of "Dave," a German. Fed up, Blake approached the bully and asked him to quit picking on the customer. "Maybe you want to take it up, you son-of-a-bitch!"

Harbour replied, "Stand back you son-of-a-bitch, or I'll put a ball through you!" At the same time, to make sure Blake understood his threat, Harbour laid his hot hand on the cool butt of his revolver. Believing that discretion was the better part of valor, Blake immediately turned and entered the bar where he hopped up and sat on the counter.

Three to five minutes later, Harbour followed Blake into the room and declared he "would lick the son-of-a-bitch before night." Apparently trying to pacify the drunken Harbour, Blake suggested, "Let's take a drink." But those words hardly cleared his mouth before Harbour's fist drove them back through Blake's teeth. Before Harbour could strike again, William Dillon, another "ranch" patron, grabbed the drunk and helped hustle him outside. Although Blake followed Harbour to the door, he apparently thought better and returned to the bar where he again plunked his butt on the counter.

Outside, still fired by the bug juice, Harbour pulled his iron and warned another customer, Regolia Herrara, that his nemesis, Blake, must die. With that, Herrara rushed inside where he warned Blake "he had better prepare himself." And prepare he did. Blake pulled a revolver from beneath the counter, hopped to the floor and he and Herrara went into the back room. As he checked to see if the gun was loaded, it accidentally discharged sending a round through the roof. Startled, but satisfied the weapon was ready, Blake put the gun into his pocket.

Through the acrid, blue smoke, the men returned to the bar where they found Harbour seated at a table. As soon as the drunk Harbour saw Blake, he muttered an obscenity and lurched for his gun. Blake drew first, however, and planted his slug some ten inches deep into the left side of Harbour's abdomen. As Harbour continued to try to pull the pistol from his holster, Blake fired a second shot, but it missed.

It is not clear exactly what happened next, but the wounded Harbour apparently tried to make his way to

Fort Laramie and had walked approximately two miles before he collapsed on the trail. However, he was found, and an ambulance was summoned to carry him the remaining one-and-a-half miles to his destination. Unfortunately for him, as well as for Blake, the wound proved fatal. Harbour died the following day at the old fort.

Blake, quickly imprisoned, was brought to trial about five months later and found "Guilty of Murder in the Second Degree." He was sent on April 8, 1872, to the House of Corrections in Detroit, Michigan, where the judge had sentenced him to imprisonment for life. He died there on November 30, 1875.

It is believed that two additional fatalities fell to violence at the Six Mile during the Black Hills gold rush and prior to 1877, but documentation concerning their circumstances has gone undetected.

THE LAST KNOWN VICTIM

While most of the killings at the hog ranches were over women, at least one was of a man on the side of the law: Adolph Cuny, the last known victim at the Six Mile, was serving as a deputy sheriff at the time of his death. He also was one of the proprietors of the Six Mile ranch.

During the summer of 1877, the Wall-Blackburn band of highwaymen committed a series of stage holdups, and a special U.S. Deputy Marshal, Charles

Hayes of Cheyenne, was appointed to capture or kill the bandits. On July 22, the gang went to the Six Mile Ranch. Just before arriving there, the gang stopped at the McCormick Place for lunch where they talked pleasantly and seemed like any ordinary customers. After lunch they went down the road to the Six Mile where they held up the place.

Hayes, upon learning of the gang's presence in the area, deputized Adolph Cuny and a Mr. Sprague to assist him. When they arrived at the ranch, Hayes sent Cuny and Sprague to the front of the establishment. Cuny was told to enter the front door while Sprague stood guard outside. In the meantime, Hayes went to the rear door where he entered through the kitchen. As soon as he saw Cuny plunge through the front entry, Hayes moved to the bar to confront Duncan "Dunc" Blackburn.

"Blackburn, I want you!" said Hayes, according to Laramie County court records.

"What for?" asked Blackburn. Hayes frisked the outlaw without replying.

Hayes told Cuny to watch the men, especially Blackburn, while he went outside to search the vicinity. If anyone moved, warned Hayes, Cuny was "to kill him." Cuny responded that he "would give Blackburn a free pass to hell, if he wanted one." Blackburn was standing with his back to the wall and between a table and the bar as Cuny, at the end of the bar, held him at bay with a rifle that was leveled at his gut.

"Deputy" Cuny apparently was so engrossed with Blackburn that he paid little attention to Clark Pelton, alias Kid Webster, one of Blackburn's henchmen. He did not hear Kid Webster enter the room. The Kid had been sleeping in the "South room" of the building, and awakened by cursing and swearing, the Kid grabbed his brass-sided, sixteen-shot Winchester and entered the adjoining barroom. His command for Cuny to step aside and release Blackburn startled the deputy. Cuny spun instantly, rushed forward and fired a wild shot at the Kid, who returned fire with one slug burying itself some twelve-inches deep in Cuny's right side. Staggering against his assailant, Cuny struggled with the Kid briefly before the deputy dropped dead on the floor. The Kid rushed outside and escaped. Blackburn and Wall immediately grabbed guns from behind the bar and went out to settle with Hayes.

Hayes, who was about one-hundred yards away, heard the shots and ran back to the building. The bar, with the exception of Cuny's body, was empty. Hayes went back outside to see what direction Blackburn and his cronies had taken, but they were nowhere in sight. Hayes was told they went towards Deer Creek. When no one would help him pursue the felons, he promptly arrested a gang member named Bowman and two other men who failed to identify Kid Webster and his cohort Wall. Leaving Sprague in charge of the prisoners, Hayes went to Fort Laramie.

Once at the fort, he telegraphed details of the incident to Sheriff Carr in Cheyenne before returning to the Six Mile with Captain Lawson and twenty of his soldiers. Blackburn, Kid Webster and Wall, however, were long gone.

During the Black Hills gold rush, at least two more men were killed at the Six Mile. The ranch, however, survived until March 1876, when it was abandoned and later converted to a stage station where "good meals" were served for fifty-cents each. They were, at least, until Jules Ecoffey died on November 26 of that year, from injuries inflicted during a fight three months earlier with a man named Stonewall. Ecoffey and Cuny had been partners in the Six Mile operation.

SOURCES CITED

In addition to Spring's excellent book, the author found Douglas C. McChristian's article "The Bug Juice War," in the *Annals of Wyoming* (Fall, 1977), a wonderful source of near-forgotten tales regarding the tribulations and trials of errant enlisted men. John D. McDermott's study of military records produced the first known reference to the Six Mile in Fort Laramie records. See Carley's "Cheyenne-Deadwood Trail Trek" in the *Annals of Wyoming* for details.

C.G. Coutant's notes from 1884-85 in the *Annals of Wyoming* article "Thomas Jefferson Carr: A Frontier Sheriff" (July, 1948) provided insight into the background regarding the Six Mile's ownership and development. McDermott's and Spring's histories supplemented this effort.

Elnora L. Frye's *Atlas of Wyoming Outlaws at the Territorial Penitentiary* (Laramie, WY: Jelm Mountain Publications, 1990) provided the first clue to the case of John Boyer. The author thanks the Wyoming Historical Research Section, too, for making available its microfilmed copies of the *Cheyenne* (WY) *Daily Evening Leader* (October 31, 1870; April 7, 8 and 21, 1871, and December 7, 1872). The color and commentary provided by those stories as well as the many details contained in Brian Jones' "John Richards, Jr. & the Killing at the Fetterman" story in the *Annals of Wyoming* (Fall, 1971) help bring history to life.

In addition to research made available by Frye's scholarship, the author was only able to tell Tousant Kensler's story by carefully studying Laramie County Criminal Case File Number 85 and Dr. Edward J. O'Callahan's April 12, 1872, Post Mortem. These may be found at the Wyoming State Archives in Cheyenne.

The setting for the killing of Cuny was provided courtesy of Virginia Cole Trenholm's *Footprints on the Frontier* (Douglas, WY: Douglas Enterprise Co., 1945). *The Black Hills Trails* (Rapid City: Rapid City Publishing, 1924) by Jesse Brown and A.M. Willard also was helpful. Sworn testimony and facts concerning the case came from Laramie County Criminal Case File Number 2-415, Territory of Wyoming vs. William Webster (real name Clark Pelton). Again, these latter records are on file at the Wyoming State Archives.

Much of the taste of this tale was drawn from such secondary sources as Doug Engebretson's *Empty Saddles, Forgotten Names: Outlaws of the Black Hills and Wyoming* (Aberdeen, SD: North Plains Press, 1982); Brown's and Willard's account, as well as the *Cheyenne (WY) Daily Sun* (May 28, 1879) in which a July 23, 1877, letter from Hayes to Sheriff T.J. Carr was published. The *Cheyenne Daily Leader* (July 25 and 26, 1877) and "Sketches from Life of James M. Sherrod of

Rawlins" in the *Annals of Wyoming* (January, 1927) also provide important details.

To understand and accurately report George Blake's murder of Perry Harbour, it was necessary to study the various official documents contained in Laramie County Criminal Case file Number 2-58. That is on file at the Wyoming State Archives. Brian Jones' research of the case is published in his article "Wild Ways and Days in Old Wyoming" which also offered little known details that had not been previously reported about these characters' lives. Jones' story appears in *The English Westerner's Society Brand Book*, (Vol. 29, No.2) published in the Summer of 1992 in London, England.

The Three Mile Hog Ranch

 DIRECTLY EAST OF THE Six Mile was another Cuny and Ecoffey establishment: the Three Mile Ranch. It was three and one-half miles down the Laramie River and southwest of Fort Laramie. Construction of the twelve to fifteen structures that constituted the ranch began there in early 1872. In the beginning, the partners built the hewn-log main building about fifty-feet square with loopholes on each side to repel Indian attacks. The ranch was just beyond the borders of the Fort Laramie military reservation on the north bank of the Laramie River.

The infamous Three Mile Hog Ranch, directly east of the Six Mile, was three and one-half miles down the Laramie River and southwest of Fort Laramie. Started as a legitimate trading post, saloon and hotel in 1872, a slack summer business forced its owners to hire some women who could attract soldiers from the fort. (Courtesy Wyoming State Museum)

East of this fortress, in early 1872, Cuny and Ecoffey erected a large store and many buildings including a warehouse, bunkhouse, ice house, blacksmith shop, billiard hall and saloon, a sod corral one hundred feet square and twelve feet high and six two-room cottages, one for each working girl. The most imposing structure was a long, low building with four doors and four windows constructed of grout, an early form of cement in which coarse gravel was used instead of sand. Its walls were more than eighteen inches thick and were plastered on the inside.

Started as a legitimate trading post, saloon and hotel, a slack summer business disappointed its Swiss owners, so they added some feminine attractions. The partners catered to soldiers from Fort Laramie, who sought companionship and escape from the doldrums of garrison life. It wasn't long before a drunken soldier painted this sign above the door of the main store: "Pay Today and Trust Tomorrow." Soon thereafter the Three Mile Ranch was put "off limits" by the military authorities and officially earned its "Hog Ranch" monicker.

In 1876, Cuny and Ecoffey advertised in the Cheyenne *Daily Leader* that their establishment boasted an "outfitting store, billiard hall, blacksmith shop, and a good corral." The owners ended their ad with the modest statement, "We Don't Blow." According to pioneer John Hunton, "They sent to Omaha and

Kansas City and other places and in a short time had their houses occupied by ten or more young women, all of whom were known as sporting characters."

Many prospectors, who had evaded the military and gone into the Black Hills, came back to the Three Mile for supplies. Gold dust began to be plentiful at the place and in November 1875, Cuny and Ecoffey sent three flasks full of gold, about $125 worth, to the editor of the *Cheyenne Leader.*

It was that same month that John Thornmahlen & Company next bought the old ranch from a man named Bottlejohn in March, 1876, and stocked it with hay and feed for the accommodation of Black Hills pilgrims. Two months later, Hank Steward, who was running the place, closed out his interest when Black Hills travel tapered off as the result of Indian troubles.

For a time Andy Ryan of Cheyenne was a partner in the Three Mile ranch, but he sold his share early in 1878. Business did not do well after 1880. Bob Osborne, a former post butcher at Fort Laramie, bought the place in September 1881. Later owners of the hog ranch included Johnny Owens and Henry Riterling.

PERSIMMONS BILL

One day while Johnny Owens owned the place, William Chambers, alias "Persimmons Bill," rode to the road ranch to drink and gamble with the other idlers. Bill worked as a herder for Malcolm Campbell,

The most imposing structure at the Three Mile Ranch was a long, low building constructed of grout, an early form of cement in which coarse gravel was used instead of sand. Its walls were more than eighteen-inches thick and were plastered on the inside. The original structure, which was later modified, had four doors and four windows. (Courtesy Wyoming State Museum)

In the beginning of the Three Mile Ranch, partners Adolph Cuny and Jules Ecoffey built the hewn-log main building about fifty feet square with loopholes on each side to repel Indian attacks. East of that fortress, they erected a large store and many buildings including a warehouse, bunk house, ice house, blacksmith shop, billiard hall and saloon, a sod corral and six cottages, one for each working girl. Still later, a single-story grout building was added. It contained a series of one-room "cribs" in which prostitutes entertained their customers. (Courtesy Wyoming State Museum)

who later distinguished himself as one of Wyoming's most prominent sheriffs.

The second morning after Bill's arrival, a Laramie County deputy sheriff rode into the ranch. After a couple of drinks of "Forty Rod Bug Juice," he announced that he was looking for a man known as Persimmons Bill. Bill was suspected of robbing Deadwood stages and of murdering at least two drivers: Johnny Slaughter and "Stuttering Brown." Bill quietly strolled over to Owens.

"I understand you have a pack of hounds here that you use for hunting," Bill remarked in a low voice.

"Yes," Owens replied, "but I don't seem to get much time around here to keep them trained. They haven't had a run for months."

"Well, that's too bad," sympathized Bill; "I haven't a thing to do. What would you say if I should take them out for awhile? Maybe we could scare up a few jack-rabbits or even an antelope."

Owens approved gladly, and soon the hunted man was galloping out of danger with his "borrowed" pack of baying dogs.

Owens kept the identity of Persimmons Bill to himself and the deputy went on his way. Only then did Bill return with the dogs and with a grin on his face.

SOURCES CITED

While McDermott's segment in "Oregon Trail Trek Number One" in the *Annals of Wyoming* (October, 1955) provided many facts that were needed to relate this story, some of the most valuable details about the Three Mile were found in the Walker Ranch: Fort Laramie, Three Mile Hog Ranch (Goshen County) application to the U.S. Department of the Interior National Park Service nominating the "Cheyenne Black Hills Stage Area" for inclusion in the National Register of Historic Places (Entry #69-04-49-0001). Hart and Spring also were cited extensively.

Robert G. David provided the story about "Persimmons Bill" in his book about *Malcolm Campbell, Sheriff* (Casper: Wyomingana, Inc., 1932).

The One Mile Hog Ranch
(aka the Hog Ranch at Fetterman)

 OF THE THREE MOST notorious hog ranches in Wyoming, perhaps the rowdiest, roughest and most dangerous of all was the terrible One Mile also called the Hog Ranch at Fetterman. It originally was built by Harry Cain just across the Platte bridge and a mile or so north of Fort Fetterman on the old Bozeman Trail. Cain, a young Texan, had helped drive cattle up the trail and had worked as a cowherder for George F. Gray near Fetterman. Not only did his whiskey business flourish, but Cain, the son of a gambler, had poker games going night and day. He eventually added a dance hall and a bawdy house which very soon acquired a tough reputation.

When Fort Fetterman was abandoned by the Army on May 11, 1882, it didn't just disappear as did most other posts. It remained as "Fetterman City" and became, almost overnight, a wild and wooly frontier town. Rowdy dance halls, saloons, stores, bawdy nests, rooming houses and cafes opened for business. "The bad element of the nearby Hartville's boom town flocked to Fetterman," recalled George Cross. "Hell was turned loose in that one-time orderly fort. There was no law or order. The whiskey was a blend of 'the River Styx and Purgatory.'"

Six months after the military was gone from the fort, John "Jack" Sanders, a "cold-blooded killer and tin-horn gambler," and his equally vicious partner, John D. Lawrence, turned the old military hospital into a dance hall. They also bought Cain's ranch. Cain claimed he had "made enough money to suit me for awhile and I want to get out while I'm still in one piece." They renamed the dance hall the One Mile, one of the few hog ranches established after an Army post was actually closed.

It soon gained a reputation as one of the worst spots in Wyoming. From the beginning, the history of the ranch was marred by violence. Outlaws, as well as freighters, visited the establishment where whiskey flowed freely, and gun-fights were ordinary occurrences.

The quiet, home-like exterior of the old hospital at Fort Fetterman masks the many terrible tales it could tell. One of the most graphic shootouts ever witnessed at a hog ranch ended here on a crude operating table. The victim did not die from the slug fired into his throat. Death came instead when that bullet slipped into the windpipe and suffocated him. (Courtesy Wyoming State Museum)

Cowboys, too, from ranches within a radius of one-hundred miles came to Fetterman to drink, gamble and revel in their spare time.

Across the Platte bridge, to the north of the post, the One Mile ranch boasted a big saloon, gambling joint and dance hall. In addition to the ranch, there was a small hotel. Both had hitching racks in front where horses were tied most of the time as cowboys and soldiers came to relieve their thirst as well as the monotony of this western outpost.

Pioneer Abe Abrahams recalled in a letter that "the cowboys...after coming in from the various roundups, would draw some money, ride south to Fetterman where they would play cards and gamble and then ride across the river to the hog ranch where in was installed generally from six to eight women. No, they were not young girls but women between the ages, I should say of twenty-five to forty-five years and, of course, their affections were negotiable."

The hog ranch, according to Abrahams, was a large, log building, fifty feet long and forty feet wide, that had a dance hall in it:

> Off to the left...was a lean-to-room where Mr. and Mrs. (Jack and Viola) Saunders [sic] lived. Along the back wall of the resort building were seven small rooms which were the private rooms of the girls who "worked"

there. In front of these room and near the private room of Mr. and Mrs. Saunders was a bar about twenty-feet long. The door of the Saunders' room opened into the space between the back of the bar and the rooms of the girls.

In the center of the main room set a huge, wood-burning stove and in the left hand corner, and front part of the room there was a table where five or six men could play cards. They played Spanish Monte. Against the right wall there was a small, elevated platform where the fiddler played for the dances. The dancing, which went on whenever there was a large enough crowd, which was most of the time, was done around the unoccupied space of the large room, around the bar; the stove; near the gamblers' table and the fiddler's platform.

Across the road—about twenty feet from the hog ranch building—Abrahams fondly recollected, was another log building, about twenty feet long and ten feet wide, that housed a five-by-ten-foot kitchen and a dining room fifteen feet long. Mr. and Mrs. Sanders and the girls and their guests ate here. The long table, covered with oil cloth, in the center of the room could accommodate about twenty people.

"There were only two chairs that I ever saw there and they were for Saunders and his wife," said Abe in one of his letters. "The girls and guests sat on benches. There was a large stable to the right of the Hog Resort where the cowboys kept their horses overnight. Every month, when the cowboys were paid, they came into Fetterman and cashed their checks at the hog ranch, and spent the greater part there before returning to the ranches where they worked. Now at one end of the cook house there was a room also logs which was always kept locked. It was a liquor room where Jack had his brother Jim tend bar for awhile."

George Cross adds his own memories of the ranch and its proprietors:

> Mrs. Sanders could drink more whiskey than any cowboy on the range.
>
> They (the partners) enlarged the "Hog Ranch" extensively, adding elaborate equipment. It flourished twenty-four hours a day as a notorious hangout for card sharks and gamblers from far and near. Every kind of "badger game" was used on the innocent, unsophisticated cowboys.
>
> In order to get to the bar a long board walk ran in front of stalls where "loose women" plied their ancient profession. A small window opened from each stall and often an

unsuspecting cowboy's Stetson hat was snatched off his head through one of these windows enroute to the bar. Reclaiming it usually increased business. This "Hog Ranch" flourished for several years as the most notorious gambling, red light house west of Chicago. Gambling for big stakes continued night and day and often herds of cattle changed hands according to the way the cards fell. Hot disputes and bigger arguments were frequent occurrences and many were decided by the barrel of a gun. It was reported that several men disappeared mysteriously and many wondered if they were victims of Sanders and Lawrence. It acquired such a bad reputation that we more conservative cowboys stayed clear of it in fear of our lives.

GOOSE EGG COWBOYS' SHOOTOUT

It was also in 1882—Monday, October 12, to be precise—when a drunken cowpuncher, who had shot a ranch bookkeeper in an argument over past pay, was hanged from the corner of a jail at the old fort. The Goose Egg ranch crew was spending the night at Fetterman after finishing the fall roundup.

J.H. "Arkansas Red" Capps, a Goose Egg cowboy, who having got a snoot full and spent his pay, badgered the firm's bookkeeper and paymaster, Dick

(Richard P.) Elgin, for twenty-five dollars. Elgin reminded Capps that he already was overdrawn on his wages. In the tussle that followed, Capps accidentally caught his heel in a knothole in the floor, fell and shot himself in the thigh. Thinking Elgin had pulled iron on him, Capps turned his .44 caliber pistol on the bookkeeper and shot him in the left side of the chin. The bullet, which proved fatal, lodged in the upper left side of the Elgin's skull.

When Capps raced from the saloon and tried to escape, he ironically grabbed Elgin's horse which subsequently threw him near the bridge over the Platte River north of Fetterman. Jumping to his feet, he saw Mike Reagon, a "tin horn gambler," riding with Bill Jaycox from the local hog ranch towards the fort. After Capps demanded Reagon's mount, the gambler drew his gun and put his spurs to his horse. But Capps sidestepped the hooves and shot the rider as he sped past. However, the wound was not fatal, and Reagon was able to get to Fetterman where a posse was formed.

Capps was caught about one hundred yards beyond the north entrance to the bridge by Sheriff Malcolm Campbell's brother, Dan, and taken to Fetterman where he was locked in the old government guardhouse.

Only two hours later that evening, Elgin's friends overpowered the guard, Tom Walker. Capps was hauled from his cell and dragged to the southwest corner of the guardhouse where a rope was thrown over a log that stuck out from the eaves and he was hanged. Apparently the vigilantes felt no animosity, because they all turned out later for a big funeral and buried Capps and Elgin side by side in the southeast side of the old abandoned fort's graveyard. Laramie County Justice of the Peace John O'Brien, who lived on LaPrele Creek, was called to hold an inquest. His verdict: Capps "came to his death by parties unknown to the jury."

A postscript to this tragedy was provided by a young remittance man from England named Craven. He had been on a spree lasting the better part of a week and, still suffering the effects, was weak, shaky and extremely nervous. Unaware of the lynching, he walked around the building, his head down, holding his hat against the Wyoming wind. Suddenly Craven bumped into something heavy and dark, which was dangling from above. The object swung out, back and hit him again. When he saw it was Capps' body, he started to run and no one ever saw him again in those parts.

THE CANNIBAL OF COLORADO

Despite the fact that One Mile was able to draw a clientele other than soldiers, the resort seemed unable to improve the caliber of its customers. The outcasts of the frontier worked and drank there. Its reputation grew so notorious that many regarded it as a sanctuary beyond the reach of the law. Alferd Packer, the feared "Colorado Cannibal" would prove this belief wrong.

This mug shot of Alferd Packer was taken upon entering the penitentiary in Canon City, Colorado, as Prisoner Number 1389. The "Colorado Cannibal" left Utah in November 1873, as a guide for a party of twenty-one enroute to the gold fields of Colorado. Five months later after surviving winter storms on a smorgasbord of five companions, he arrived in the Los Pinas Indian Agency where it was reported he was "fat and had plenty of money." (Courtesy Colorado State Historical Society Museum)

During the winter of 1873, Packer and a party of twenty-one men trekked out of Bingham Canyon near Provo, Utah, for the gold fields of Colorado. A winter blizzard swept through forcing Packer and five of his companions to hole up in a narrow valley. The rest escaped. After the storm blew itself out, only one man walked out—Alferd Packer. He arrived at the Los Pinas Indian Agency, west of Lake City, Colorado, on April 16, 1874, "fat and had plenty of money." After admitting he had killed—and eaten—five of his prospecting party to avoid starvation, he was arrested and jailed at Saguache. He subsequently escaped less than five months later and successfully eluded the law nearly nine years before he was discovered at the hog ranch near Fort Fetterman.

On March 10, 1883, Jean Cazabon, a French itinerant peddler of household notions stopped at Billie and Ellie Brown's hog ranch on LaPrele Creek. "Little Frenchie," as he was called because of his small stature, was enroute from Cheyenne to Fetterman. The place was crowded and noisy. As "Frenchie" related the experience to his friend George Cross:

> A prospector named John Swartz was also staying there. We were introduced and something unpleasantly familiar struck me about this so-called Swartz. After some mental reflection I recognized him as Packer, the

cannibal, however, I was nonchalant and didn't make known my suspicions as I wanted to be absolutely certain.

Swartz had acquired false teeth and had grown a mustache which had changed his appearance considerably, but it was the man's voice that kept ringing in my ears. I went over and over in my mind and I recalled that same voice that had spoken those gruesome words of "how sweet human flesh tasted."

The last time the two men had met, Packer had vowed to kill Cazabon on sight. But now the "man-eater" failed to recognize his nemesis, one of the twenty-one men with whom he had left Utah for the gold fields back in the the late fall of 1873.

I continued to quietly concentrate and finally confirmed my suspicions when I saw his hands. Packer had stubs for two fingers on his left hand. Now I was certain that this man at large was the same demon who possessed those hideous unnatural, murderous qualities of a mad man and savage cannibal!

I was frightened for my life but I had to be a good actor. Fortunately, Packer didn't show any signs of recognition toward me

Famed Fetterman lawman, Sheriff Malcolm Campbell walked one of the wildest beats in the Old West. Where success meant surviving a bullet, Malcolm outwitted and outlived the worst of the bunch. He captured the feared hog ranch patron Al Packer, for example, and returned him to justice after the "Colorado Cannibal" evaded his home state authorities for nearly ten years. The sheriff also put a lock on the infamous One Mile's door to hasten an end to the hog ranch era in Wyoming. (Courtesy Wyoming State Museum)

and he asked me to bring him some blasting powder for his prospecting on my next trip. I handed him my order book to write out what he wanted and sign it, which he did as John Swartz.

Continuing his tale, "Frenchie" told Cross that, because of the storm raging outside, Brown's hog ranch was crowded:

> ...so I rolled out my bed on the kitchen floor and crawled in with all my clothes on and didn't dare to even think of sleeping a wink. I kept my pocket knife open in my hand and at 4 o'clock (in the morning) I quietly slipped out, hitched my team to my wagon and raced them all the way to Fort Fetterman, feeling mighty lucky to still be alive.

Without attracting attention, Cazabon sought out Deputy Sheriff Malcolm Campbell at Fetterman and told him his story. Campbell knew the man who called himself Swartz. Only two months earlier Swartz got himself drunk at the One Mile notorious bawdy house across the North Platte River from Fetterman. When he subsequently ordered a meal and the waiter was not fast enough for him, Packer threatened the poor man with a pistol. Sheriff Campbell was called and he jailed Swartz overnight in the old fort guardhouse. He was released when the frightened waiter refused to press charges.

This time the sheriff checked with his counterpart in Laramie and quickly received instructions to arrest Packer. Campbell and his brother, Dan, rode out in a buckboard to Emanuel "Crazy Horse" George's cabin on Latham Creek, a tributary of muddy Wagon Hound Creek. They hid in the brush trying to decide upon the best method of attack when Packer walked out of the cabin unarmed to the nearby creek for a bucket of water. They grabbed him and put handcuffs on him. Packer said, "That's the first time in ten years I haven't had my gun on me. You'd have never got me." They took their criminal to the old fort and from there to Cheyenne where Packer was delivered to Sheriff Clair Smith of Hinsdale County, Colorado. Smith and his prisoner continued on to Denver that afternoon.

Packer's departure, however, did little to diminish the hog ranch's reputation for harboring the lawless, the lushes, as well as those with overactive libidos.

Another character included in this mix was "Tobacco Jake." It will come as no surprise that he was named for the brown juice that ran from and stained the corners of his mouth. A hard drinker, who later in his life became a dope addict, Jake was shot while on a drunken spree. As the wound was being dressed, the local sawbones, Dr. Amos Barber, tried to impress upon the victim the seriousness of such foolishness.

"Listen, Jake," said Doc Barber, "that narrow escape should be a lesson to you. If that bullet had gone an inch farther to the right, it would have gone into your brain." "Hell, Doc," countered Jake, "if it had gonna *quarter* of an inch to the left, it would'a missed me altogether." Barber, incidentally, later moved to Cheyenne where he was elected Secretary of State in Wyoming's first statewide election. He subsequently became Acting Governor and served from 1890 to 1893 when Wyoming's first governor Francis E. Warren was elected to the U.S. Senate.

THE NOTORIOUS SANDERS

Of all the characters who frequented the One Mile ranch, one of the most interesting was the co-owner Sander's wife, Viola. "Vi," as she was called, was "a pretty woman and the cowboys who frequented the resort found that the only way they could get to talk to her was to buy two drinks of her husband's liquor, then she would take one glassful and drink with the buyer." It was often said that she drank twenty or thirty drinks in succession with men who would have fallen to the floor dead drunk before they could have taken half as many.

Although she admitted to using a technique similar to that of Ellie Brown, she gave it her own distinctive twist. After taking a swig of whiskey from a clear glass, she would spit it into a empty dark, frosted glass, which allegedly contained her chaser. Then she would quickly

Early Wyoming Governor Amos Barber spent much of his early career as a physician and "specialist on social diseases" treating hog ranch customers near Fetterman. At the insistence of one such patron, he even consented, at gunpoint, to brush his patient's teeth—with Barber's own toothbrush. (Courtesy Wyoming State Museum)

put both glasses back on the waiter's tray so that he could carry them away before anyone was the wiser.

Jack Sanders himself was quite a character. He, too, went into Doc Barber's office at Fetterman one day and said, "I understand that you clean teeth. I want a job done." Barber, a "specialist on social diseases," told him that he was not a dentist. He could prescribe, however, some form of tooth powder. Sanders drew his gun and told the good doctor, "You son-of-a-bitch, you clean my teeth or I'll blow your head off!" Dr. Barber immediately brought out his own toothbrush and cleaned Sanders' "dirty, decayed, tobacco stained teeth" and charged him five-dollars for the job. "Both were satisfied."

Abe Abrahams had his own special memory of Jack. During Abe's "cowboy" days, he recalled riding over to the "ranch" one morning:

> It seems I was just in time for breakfast, for...the girls did not get up very early, and I, of course, joined them being young and always hungry. Jack Sanders was sitting at the head of the table with Vi along side. There were two other men beside myself and as I remember six girls?
>
> It was a real nice meal, baking powder biscuits, fired meat, Arbuckles coffee etc.... The meat was on one large platter and was passed

around after eating awhile someone [Sanders] said, this is elk.

...Sanders had an impediment in his speech but he said nothing more. Pretty soon someone at the other end of the table said please pass the beef. Pulling out his six gun and shooting into the ceiling he [Sanders] said I said this is elk, and from the end of the table came a calm voice saying, would you please pass me the elk.

Sanders' inference seems clear that the "elk" probably had been someone's branded stock.

THIS FENEX FAILED TO RISE; IT WAS "ASHES TO ASHES..."

Another killing at the Fetterman hog ranch was recalled by Malcolm Campbell, the later famed sheriff, who was a "deputy" when the shooting happened on August 29, 1884.

A few days before the tragedy, "Tallow Man" Harry Crosby, John Fenex and "Pretty Boy" Frank Wallace had visited the ranch where they rode their horses into the saloon and began shooting holes in the ceiling. They also shot through a bedroom door, blew out the windows and put a few slugs into the large mirror back of the bar. Yelling and laughing hilariously, they terrorized the "working girls" as the patrons ducked for cover.

Sanders and Lawrence, the proprietors of the ranch, threw Crosby, Fenex and Wallace out of their bar and warned there would be serious trouble if they came back to the ranch. One bright, calm day two weeks later, however, the cowpokes decided to return to the One Mile. Campbell saw the cowboys before they left for the ranch, but was unsuccessful in getting them to go home "and keep out of trouble."

Campbell was relaxing, at his home at Fetterman, enjoying the bright, calm day, when he heard gun shots at the hog ranch and soon saw Fenex astride a white horse with a man on each side of him holding him on his horse. Fenex had been shot in the stomach "and was done for." But Sanders and Lawrence were still in hot pursuit. They "rode up as fast as their horses could bring them," Mrs. Campbell remembered in an interview. "They were white with rage."

Lawrence, with a wound in his shoulder, still carried his shotgun. Sanders had two six-guns. "By the time they reached the hotel," said Mrs. Campbell, "I, with my baby clasped in my arms, got to them as soon as they stopped their horses. I was crying and begging them not to kill Malcolm. Saunders said, 'No, Mrs. Campbell; we won't hurt Malcolm, but he has got to give up Ferris' [Whether by error or design to protect the sensitivities of the Fenex family, Mrs. Campbell incorrectly identified Fenex as Ferris.]

"Malcolm was standing in the door, gun in hand.

He cautioned them not to come a step nearer, but they told him he had to give up Ferris [Fenex], that they were going to come in and get him and finish him. I shall never forget the defiant look he [Malcolm] gave them when he said, 'The only way you will get in here will be over my dead body.' So they calmed down and went with him."

Witnesses said later that they had seen Fenex and Lawrence engaged in a "long talk" at the bar when suddenly Fenex pulled leather and shot both Lawrence and Ella Wilson, "a common prostitute," in their shoulders. In the melee that followed, Wallace fired at customers George Beldan and Charles Heinrichs, who he seemed to suspect as friends of the bar's owners.

Testifying under oath from his death bed, Fenex said he did not know who fired first, that "Lawrence had taunted and threatened him, saying he would give him twenty dollars to spit in his face." The last thing Fenex remembers was that "Lawrence and Sanders had shot at him, Lawrence hitting him in the stomach." Crosby, Fenex and Wallace decided to "go down fighting," emptying their pistols at their adversaries. Although mortally wounded, Fenex was able to escape.

Nearly simultaneously, Wallace cleared the door before he was hit by Lawrence's shotgun blast in the right eye, face, hand and scalp. Lawrence went to Wallace, who lay in the dirt, and raised his head. Wallace neither spoke nor moved, feigning death until Sanders and Lawrence left for the fort in search of Fenex. Then he got on his horse and raced to an old building in the area where he hid until a search party found him. Crosby was only slightly wounded and escaped to the E.S. Ranch, where the trio had planned to winter.

The day after the fracas, an inquest was held at John O'Brien's ranch where Lawrence was charged with attempted murder of Fenex and Wallace. He pled "not guilty." The jury referred him to Laramie where he was tried and acquitted. Fenex's wound was fatal, however, and he died four days later (September 3, 1884) in Doc Barber's old Fort Fetterman hospital bed.

In October, 1884, Lawrence, his partner Jack Sanders, and Ella Wilson, charged Frank Wallace with attempted murder. However, the case was dismissed "because of lack of material witnesses including cowhand Jeff Peters who had gone to Texas to spend the winter with his people and would not be back until sometime during the month of February next." Lawrence, finally took all the blame for the shooting, but he, too, was tried and acquitted.

A Diamond in the Dust

Another unlucky Fetterman City hog ranch customer was Thomas Diamond. He was gambling at Sanders and Lawrence's One Mile Hog Ranch "across the river" on October 26, 1884, when an argument broke out. Seems as though Diamond was not able to pay off his gambling debts to the two proprietors. One angry word led to another until Diamond and Sanders fired at each other. Diamond, as slow with his gun as he was with paying his bills, died on the spot with eight fatal shotgun pellets in his left breast and three more in the shoulder.

An inquest was held at the ranch site one mile north of the fort with Sam Slaymaker acting as coroner. The verdict: Sanders shot Diamond in self-defense. "Court dismissed."

THE HOG RANCH AT FETTERMAN ENDS WITH A "BANG"

Pioneer Abe Abrahams recalled that Sanders finally abandoned the old hog ranch and went in partnership with a man named William "Billy" Bacon. They built another one of native lumber on the Fetterman side of the river about one-half mile out. "It was a big structure built of the same lines as the log one on the other side of the river," said Abrahams, but he couldn't remember when it was constructed.

Their infamous hog ranch at Fetterman finally came to an end on November 30, 1885, when the partners got into an argument and mortally wounded one another.

Billy Bacon was born in Iowa about 1852. According to pioneer C.W. Horr, "Bacon came to LaBonte in about '79 and ran a road ranch at the crossing. Just

squatters right. Sold his right to Harry Pollard's father
in the Spring of '83 for $5,000. Then he went to
Cheyenne and was drinking and gambling, but some
of his friends got him to leave, so he went back to
LaBonte and bought a bunch of cows. He took the
cows up to Bacon Park in June, '84. I saw him there.
He had built a cabin and his wife was there in '85 or
'86. He traded the cattle to Frank Gore—100 head—
for Frank's Saloon in Fetterman."

Bacon and Sanders subsequently became partners
in what John Lawrence testified was called the One
Mile Hog Ranch or, sometimes simply the "Hog
Ranch at Fetterman." Lawrence had known Sanders
for about two years and had been his partner in a pre-
vious hog ranch venture. That relationship would
come unraveled on December 9, 1885.

The first loose thread was snagged as the partners
were "figuring at their books." Witness John Worth
testified that they had several arguments, but "finally
settled them and both went over to the hog ranch.
Bacon appeared to be angry. He walked off. I supposed
he went home."

Along about 9:15 or so that evening, Bacon
returned to the ranch. He "appeared friendly," to most
of the eight people who crowded the bar. Most of
them sat on benches or in chairs, hugging the stove to
ward off the winter chill that seeped through the dry
wood walls. At some point in the conversation, Vi

Sanders groused that there not enough girls to fill "assignments."

The implication was that there would be more money in the till if Bacon had done a better job of getting more girls to come up on the train from Cheyenne. Bacon seemed to handle her sharp tongue in good humor, as he joked with her briefly then left the building. But within about fifteen minutes, Bacon returned. He had a burr under his saddle and was obviously angry. Storming up to Jack, who was sitting with his wife, Vi, on a bench near the stove, Bacon said, "Sanders, did you ever say you could get away [*sic*] with me?" Or words to that effect.

> "No, I did not say so," answered Jack. But Bacon wasn't appeased: "I think you did say so for I have been told you said so."
> Vi Sanders interjected, "Mr. Bacon, Sanders never said so" to which Bacon said, with a cut, "I would not take your word under oath."
> "Bacon, hold on!" countered Sanders; "Don't go too fast. Whoever told you I said so is a damned liar."
> "I think you did say so," replied Bacon, "but you can't get the drop on me."

With that, Bacon slapped Jack's cheek. Jack sprang from the bench where he had been sitting and went for his attacker. Vi, at nearly the same time, jumped up to protect her husband, who she thought was unarmed. As she pushed between the men, she tried unsuccessfully to grab the handle of Bacon's gun that protruded from the waistband of his pants. Bacon pushed her to the side and shot Jack in the gut above and to the right of the navel. As Bacon fired again, Jack jumped towards the bar, fell to the floor, but was able to pull a gun from his own waistband. According to Worth, that is where he usually carried it. While leaning on his arm, he twice tried to shoot at Bacon, but the gun "snapped" (misfired) both times. Jack's third shot struck Bacon in the throat.

Jack, with his pistol still in his right hand, quickly crawled to his feet as Vi joined him to retreat down the hall where he fell. Vi ran into her room. She knew he was "hurt bad and expected to die." The wounded Bacon followed them into the hall to fire another shot from near the door.

As Vi came out of her room, she found Jack getting up off the floor.

Bacon struggled out of the door and told Louis Burr, who was standing nearby, "I'm shot bad; I wish you'd take me home."

In the meantime, Jack had started to follow Bacon and Burr down the street when Vi came out and pulled her spouse back into the house. He soon returned to the street—this time "bareheaded" and armed with a shotgun. Approaching the front of the building where Bacon lived, he yelled. When John Ryan came to the door, Jack asked, "Where is Bacon?" Ryan told him he was upstairs in bed..."shot." With that, Jack "kind of reeled and staggered off the sidewalk" and said, "Someone come take me home. I'm shot."

Lawrence, who witnessed the action, walked up to Jack and disarmed him. Jack said he was "shot through the belly" and could not live. "I went home with him," said Lawrence.

Louis Burr, after getting Bacon settled, went back to the hog ranch where he found Jack Sanders "standing with his hand up against the door with his coat off." Burr and Lawrence "helped undress him (and) found him wounded in the abdomen above (the) waist band of (his) trousers." As Vi bathed the bullet wound in his belly, word was sent to find a doctor. After he was put to bed, Sanders complained repeatedly that someone had tampered with his pistol—if it had not "snapped," he would not have been shot. Witness Charlie Cobb and S. Mortimer, who subsequently examined Sander's revolver, could find no evidence to substantiate those allegations.

Lawrence said he was with Jack Sanders until he died, between four and five the following day, December 10.

During a subsequent operation at Stockman's Hospital at the fort to try to save Bacon, four men were needed to hold him on the operating table as Dr.

Watkins, a surgeon who had been called from Fort McKinney near Buffalo, prepared to probe for the bullet. As the men pinned Bacon down while the doctor administered ether, the patient's struggle dislodged a lead slug which choked him to death when it slipped down his windpipe.

His friend George Cross recalled that, "As he was lowered into the ground an old freighter offered up this prayer: 'O God, if there is a God, have mercy on Billy's soul, if he has a soul. Amen.' Someone remarked, 'His body will never rot as it is pickled in whiskey.'" It is believed that Bacon was buried beside Sanders in the southeast corner of the Fort Fetterman Cemetery.

This last killing at the One Mile gave the authorities cause to close the hog ranch for good. The man who put the padlock on the hog ranch's door was the same Sheriff Campbell who arrested Alferd Packer.

SOURCES CITED

In addition to Robert G. David's work *Malcolm Campbell, Sheriff*, the author pulled extensively from Sharon Lass Field's "Fort Fetterman Cemetery" pamphlet (Wyoming Recreation Commission, 1970) to separate fact from fiction. For additional biographical information regarding Sanders, the author recommends the *Buffalo* (WY) *Big Horn Sentinel* (December 12, 1885), which contains specifics regarding his background while living there.

For an understanding of the culture and the times, it is helpful to read Mrs. Malcolm Campbell's memoirs as recorded in a January 6, 1939, interview that is on file at the Wyoming Historical Research Section, Department of Commerce, Cheyenne, WY.

George H. Cross's "Wyoming Long Ago" article in the *Wyoming State Tribune* (July 30, 1939) offers a snapshot concerning the physical characteristics of the One Mile. For perhaps the best description of the ranch and its habitues, however, no one tells it better than Abrahams in his December 12, 1939, letter to Agnes W. Spring as well as in his January 29, February 4, and March 6, 1940, notes to Rowley; this correspondence is on file at the Wyoming Historical Research Section.

The ultimate insight and facts concerning the bloody Goose Egg Ranch cowboy's shootout, however, are only available through research of Albany County Criminal Case File Number 22. And, the running gunfight and tragic death of Fenex perhaps is best understood through the study of Albany County Criminal Court Case Files Number 203 and Number 219. Also, William H. Barton's remarks entitled, "The Shady Ladies and the Scarlet Arts of the West" is an excellent primer on hog ranches in general. All these documents are on file at the Wyoming State Archives in Cheyenne. C.W. Horr's May 4, 1950, letter to Clark Bishop in Carley's "Oregon Trail Trek Number Two," as published in the *Annals of Wyoming* (April, 1956), provides specifics not found elsewhere concerning the Fenex incident while the *Cheyenne* (WY) *Democratic Leader* (September 2, 1885) helps flesh out that affair.

If there are experts on Al Packer, they must be Fred and Jo Mazzulla of Denver, CO, authors of *Al Packer, A Colorado Cannibal* (Denver: privately published, 1968). Robert W. Fenwick's "Alfred [*sic*] Packer: The True Story of the Man Eater" (Denver: *The Denver Post*, 1964) ranks second only to the Mazzula's extensively illustrated and highly detailed booklet, although Fenwick errs by misspelling Packer's first name. An interview with Cheyenne-based historian Sharon Lass Field produced additional, unusual facts as provided by her grandfather, Emanuel George. George employed Packer near Fort Fetterman.

Vi Sanders's account of how she "out drank" her customers, was gained courtesy of George Cross's excellent research and writings.

For the definitive account of the double-death of Sanders-Bacon, it is most important to review the extensive sworn inquest testimony as contained in Albany County Criminal Case Case Number 58. Abrahams' letters of February 4 and 29, 1940, to Rowley elaborate the tragedy.

Epilogue

As quickly as they came, the hog ranches suddenly were gone with the men they served. Like dry tumbleweeds, torn from their taproots and blown out of sight, the hog ranches are a memory at best. The only things left to mark their place in history are some shards of colored glass. Here and there a rusty iron hoop from a whiskey keg breaks the crusty soil near a decaying foundation. And, of course, there are those few small unmarked graves that hold the once bright dreams of hog ranch gals and their customers.

Index

photo by
Craig Pindell

ABOUT THE AUTHOR

LARRY K. BROWN (1936-), a fourth generation journalist, earned a degree in Journalism from the University of Nebraska in 1960 before entering the U.S. Air Force where he spent the next twenty years as a Public Affairs officer. He graduated from Boston University in 1970 with a Master of Science degree in Public Relations and Mass Communications and later earned predoctorate credits.

In 1985 he joined Sun Exploration and Production as Director, Public Relations and Communications. Eight years later Brown went to work for the American Heart Association (AHA) and in 1988 moved to Cheyenne as the Executive Director, AHA-Wyoming, Inc.

His writing credits include more than 800 newspaper, magazine and encyclopedia articles plus a two-hour *Today Show* aired in 1979 by NBC-TV and a one-hour *Prime Time Sunday* script broadcast the following year by ABC-TV about Strategic Air Command's underground command and control center.

Since 1992 he has written exclusively about Western history. His forthcoming book *You Are Respectfully Invited to Attend My Execution* will also be published by High Plains Press. The latter book contains the little known stories of the seven men who were legally executed in the Wyoming Territory.

Brown, a Wyoming State Historical Society volunteer, also writes "In Old Wyoming," a regular series for the Society's *Wyoming Annals* magazine.

The cover illustration of the softcover edition is
by Professor Henry Worrall and is from the book
*Historic Sketches of the Cattle Trade
of the West and Southwest*
(Ramsey, Millett & Hudson, Printers, 1874)
It was color enhanced by artist B. J. Durr.

Two hundred copies were bound in cloth
as a limited edition for collectors.
No additional cloth copies will be manufactured.

*The text is composed in
twelve point Adobe Garamond.
Display type is Post Antiqua BE and Rosewood.
The book is printed on
sixty-pound Gladtfelter Supple Opaque
acid-free, recycled paper
by Thomson-Shore.*